TESTIMONIALS

Maree brings decades of experience, both hers, and the women whose stories she shares. She takes you on a journey of insight, discovery and clarity to help you blast through your ceiling. Her commitment for supporting women in regional Australia to step out and step up, to live a full life, gives the reader the same opportunity. Maree provides a practical guide to help you move towards action designed by you. Grab a notebook, your favourite hot drink, and get ready to create your future.

Pollyanna Lenkic, author of Women & Success: Redefining what matters most at home, at work and at play.

This book is a practical guide. I recognise the different phases and stages people I know are at. The personal stories of rural women are motivating and engaging.

Alanna Bastin-Byrne, Femeconomy.

In *The Grass Ceiling*, Maree shares stories and insights into the challenges and opportunities faced by women in regional Australia. She explores the subject with sensitivity and care whilst providing practical strategies and exercises which, frankly, are not just for women in rural regions, but for women everywhere who want to break through the grass or glass. Maree brings a depth to this topic based on years of personal experiences that she shares with a level of vulnerability that connects and inspires.

Donna McGeorge, author of Making Work Work: How to get your people to show up, play nicely and get the job done.

Cutting through the grass ceiling

CUTTING THROUGH THE GRASS CEILING

WOMEN CREATING POSSIBILITY IN REGIONAL AUSTRALIA

Maree McPherson

First published in 2017 by Baker Street Press | Melbourne
All rights reserved. No part of this publication may be reproduced
by any means without the prior written consent of the publisher.

This book uses case studies to reinforce the meaning
behind its relevant chapters. Names have been omitted
or changed to protect individual privacy.

Every effort has been made to trace (and seek permission for use
of) the original source of material used within this book. Where
the attempt has been unsuccessful, the publisher would be pleased
to hear from the author/publisher to rectify any omission.

Typeset by BookPOD
Photo credit: Sue Tanian at Informal Photography

National Library of Australia Cataloguing-in-Publication entry

Title: Cutting through the grass ceiling: women creating
possibility in regional Australia / Joanna Yardley, editor.

ISBN: 9780994321497 (paperback)

Subjects: Rural women–Australia–Social conditions.
Rural women–Employment–Australia.
Women in the professions–Australia.

Other Creators/Contributors: Yardley, Joanna, editor.

There were mixed views about adding 5 girls to an all-male tribe. We had to build a cart. We had to run through waterholes and carry the cart through creeks. We would get messy. We had to stop at checkpoints and answer general knowledge questions about Scouting, and undertake tasks like tying knots.

Later that night, when we walked on stage to collect our trophy for 1st prize in the Scouting Knowledge section, we were cheered.

DEDICATIONS

To Beth and Jan: the two people who created me. You never questioned a single thing I thought I could do, except to ask how I planned to go about it. Then you backed the plan.

To my most cherished mentor, Barb. I was 28 when I first met you. I wanted to be just like you when I grew up. You seemed feisty, centred, self-aware, ethical, and fun. Over the many years we have known each other, I've found you to be all those things, and more. I love every moment we spend together, and I want there to be many more.

To my nieces, Jillian and Angela, and my great-nieces, little Andy-Jo and baby Penny.

To my 'daughters' from other mothers: Caitlin, Madison, Monique, Maddie, Lucy, Matilda, and Luiza. The world will change exponentially in your life-times. Everything will be disrupted— much of it for the better. Aspire high, and love well.

ACKNOWLEDGEMENTS

Thank you for reading this book. I have loved writing it. It means a great deal to me that you are invested enough to read it, because it means you are valuing yourself, and you want to make a difference in the world. That's the biggest thanks I can ever receive.

I thank the women who gave up their time to be interviewed. It was tough to decide who to write about. I had a long list, and not everyone said yes. Jess, Cathy, Jenny, Leah, Mel, Lynda, Angela, Robbie and Kate—thank you all for allowing me to tell your stories and for your generosity of spirit. Your bravery will inspire many (and already does).

I am indebted to the other women you will meet on reading this book. They are women I have worked with in my practice. They are not identified, and their stories are real. I know I have learned as much, if not more, from them than they have from me. Their experiences have contributed richly to my thoughts and the development of the models and exercises in the book. Coaching and mentoring them has enhanced my practice, and strengthened my skills.

I note the importance and power of education in this book. I was a good student, yet I was bored often, and the system and I didn't quite fit together. There are a handful of teachers, especially in my senior school years, who showed me possibility. One in particular never gave up nudging me in the direction he knew I could go. I'm sure he engineered things so I never got the jobs I applied for each mid-year. He convinced me with words and actions to stay and finish school. I saw him in early 2017, and thanked him personally. Another teacher gently coaxed me through a subject I was failing in HSC. She never allowed me to think I would fail. She knew the power of 'yet' and mindset before they were written about. By end-of-year exams, it was my strongest subject. These teachers taught me about grit and perseverance. In a way, this book comes from that learning.

From my early 20s, I have been positioned, by mostly women, and several men in my workplaces who saw something in me that could inspire others. I will always be thankful for the opportunity to lead a regional community services agency. This experience exposed me to some of the most enriching, hilarious, spiritual, sad, and frightening times in my life. The support I received from the CEO and executive through to the team in Gippsland, enabled me to flourish and thrive.

In 2001, I undertook the Gippsland Community Leadership Program. At the time of my selection interview, I was asked why I considered myself someone who would benefit from the program, when I'd already been in a regional leadership role for several years. I think my answer was along the lines that I could give back to others, and likely learn more at the same time. This turned out to be true in so many ways. The Program helped me take what some saw as a sideways step. It started me off in a new direction, working with people and industries I'd not been exposed to before.

My career in regional development was rich and wonderful. Again, it was the people who made it so. The men and women on the board I worked for, and the staff team, remain some of the people I've had the deepest connections with in my working life. They introduced me to the real possibility within me, and helped me shape that job into everything I wanted it to be. In that role, I was also offered my first executive coaching program. My coach transformed the way I worked and it was from her that I came to understand the power of great coaching. She was around in my life again when I was recruited to my next job, and I will always be indebted to her for her wisdom and care.

Two regional women tapped me on the shoulder for that next job. I thank them for alerting me to new possibility, which took me to a State-wide peak body as the CEO. The men and women I worked with backed my judgement. They supported me through some trying days, and into the heights of that association's great work. I am very thankful to have served successive boards, and a woman President who opened up my thinking even further. Now, as an upper house Victorian State MP, she inspires me from another perspective.

In 2013, as I was preparing to depart that job, I enrolled in an executive coaching course at Swinburne University. I found I had moved almost full circle, back to my roots in social welfare studies. I was at home, and finally felt like my next step was visible. I went on to complete my graduate studies in organisational and workplace coaching while I worked part-time back in the public sector, and did some consulting.

In late 2015, I opened my own practice. This coincided with me enrolling in Thought Leaders Business School. I thank Matt Church for founding the program, and enabling so many of us to create our own futures. I acknowledge Peter Cook for his leadership of the School, and his authenticity. My two mentors, Corrinne Armour and Donna McGeorge, have cajoled me through the authoring of this book, including a time when I accidentally deleted 12,000 words of the first manuscript. L-Plate authors make interesting errors. So many thought-leading women and men are a part of my life now, and support me in so many ways. Thank you, tribe.

My editor, Joanna Yardley, has supported me from my very first blog post to the conclusion of this book. Jo, you are clever, decisive, kind, and witty. I'm glad there are editors on the planet, and I'm very thankful to have you. You have also helped me create possibility.

The most special people in my life are saved for last. My best friends are women I lost touch with for a while when our lives went in different directions. In crises and in grief, they were always there, and in the happiest moments. Yet time seemed to get in the way of regular connection. In the past few years I've recognised those friends have never left my pit crew, and I've never left theirs. They still believe in me and my possibility—perhaps even more than I know. While other friends have come and gone, these people have stayed the distance. Whenever I have wondered if I could write a book or run a practice, they are the people cheering me on. I love you and your magical offspring. You warm my soul.

My beautiful family. What was once two parents and three siblings has grown to four nephews, two nieces, their wonderful partners, five great-nephews, and two great-nieces. We are a clan, and I derive such love and self-worth from knowing you all.

Warren, my husband and friend for so long. You're the primary reason for it all. I love keeping this going with you by my side. Every day with you is like the first walk in the sea together, holding hands. We knew then. We know now.

And to me. You've always wondered. You've always asked what would happen if you backed yourself and gave it a crack. You have worked so hard. And here it is. I'm so proud of you.

CONTENTS

INTRODUCTION

'You can't be what you can't see.'

(Hannah Riley Bowles – *Designing Gender Equality in Organisations*)

This book isn't for everyone; it will appeal mostly to a certain audience. That's deliberate.

I am a committed feminist and there are feminist references in this book. I have been criticised for being a feminist many times, and I've also been praised for it. Often, feedback comes from people who don't know what it means. Feminism has been defined in so many ways so often in the last decades; is it any wonder people aren't sure? The successes of feminism have many parents. My intent is that this book honours the philosophy of the elders, like Gloria Steinem, who famously said, 'A feminist is anyone who recognizes the equality and full humanity of women and men.'

We know that regional economies prosper when women work. Women's participation in the labour market in regional economies adds value, and keeps regional areas economically stable.

In her introduction to Sheryl Sandberg's book *Lean In*, Belinda Hutchinson[1] states that Australia needs to lift its productivity. She says that if Australian women equalled the workforce participation of men, we could add 13% to GDP. To me, it is even more important for regional Australian women to increase their labour-force participation. Women in regional areas can help grow local economies and create jobs by their expenditure on services and goods when they are part of the workforce.

It's also true that regional Australia is often at the forefront of structural adjustment. There is, and will continue to be, a changing demographic in the labour market. In regions, such as Geelong and the Latrobe Valley, men are leaving manufacturing and mining jobs, while their partners are moving back into full-time work and becoming the primary breadwinners; their spouses now retrain or take part-time employment.

Sandberg dedicates a whole chapter of her book to what she calls the Ambition Gap. 'She is very ambitious' is not a compliment in our culture, she writes. We have a different problem in regional Australia. The Aspiration Gap is a genuine problem for our economic growth. Educational and career aspiration in regional schools is demonstrably lower, and educational participation of regional young people requires additional support.[2]

. . . .

My passion is to help younger women in regional Australia step out onto the manicured lawn in their careers.

When we hold girls back, when we keep them from developing their own self-confidence, and when we dampen their aspirations, we are turning our backs on their full humanity. (We are short-selling boys at the same time.) I want girls in regional schools to know they have choices. I want their teachers to set encouraging and hopeful examples of their futures. I want them to understand how a growth mindset can impact beyond the classroom, and affect the choices they make throughout their lives.

The compelling reason (as if we need one) to lift girls' aspirations is that we know employed women enjoy greater financial independence, more stable relationships, and overall better health. It's not enough for regional and rural girls to be told they will meet someone nice and settle down to be looked after. Lack of choice from sexually transmitted debt, or because someone else holds the purse strings closed, is not an attractive option. With the burden of disease often being so much higher in regional areas compared to their city sisters, this becomes even more critical for regional women.

Yet, too many of us still lack confidence to put ourselves forward. We still encounter startling misogyny and barriers from men in positions of influence. In 2016, in response to the Victorian Government's call for 50% female representation on its statutory boards, I was told that a prominent man said that he doubted they would fill that quota, as there just weren't enough capable women to do the jobs. Yes, 2016. It's utterly astounding.

But I'm going to be controversial. While I vehemently disagree with this man and men like him, there are far too few of us who step forward. When I was recently approached for a role on a regional board, I almost stepped back. I'm an educated, confident, and highly experienced woman with significant capability in my field, yet I almost decided it was too hard to put my hand up. If it's difficult for me, how difficult is it for others?

....

This book is not so much an exploration of the women's ambition gap as it is a study of the long history of rural and regional women who have just got on with it, without billions of dollars. They have embraced feminist ideology, sometimes without even knowing it, or before the term was coined. In my view, they have lived to their full humanity.

In her book *Lean Out*, a reaction to Sandberg's quite simplistic assessment of the challenges facing women striving for gender equity, Dawn Porter describes ambition without realism as megalomania.[3] I understand what Porter means, but ambition of itself is no sin or fault. Ambition to be content with our choices and feeling like a choice has been made, is surely a worthy ambition.

Not all of us have to fight society every day, every hour, every minute. In fact, if we each do just one thing in our step towards change, that's a huge groundswell in better gender representation and equity.

The fuller life that exists outside of work and family, such as a civil life, a political life, or an emotional or spiritual life, is also part of a full being, and choices exist here too. There is also the choice not to have a family, and all the freedom that provides to women.

The women I've written about here are not the '1% feminists' we claim to be the stand-outs. These are regional women who have assisted other women, and who have helped others up the ladder by going back down to grab them by the hand. They have advocated for change by demonstrating cleverness, visibility, recognition and quiet support.

There are many examples of regional women who have cut through the grass ceiling. Women like former Qantas board chair, Margaret Jackson, who grew up and was educated in Warragul, Victoria. What is it about these women that enables them to achieve their aspirations?

I want women to recognise that this is about choice and options. Not everyone wants to be Chair of the board, CEO of BHP Billiton, or running a national peak body. Some of us do. I want women to have the self-belief and confidence to enable this to happen; to know what support we require, and be able to access it.

Like Porter, I expect you're thinking – "They're not like me ... they've had privileges I don't have", "Capitalist society is geared towards keeping us out", "Working-class women don't have these choices".

In some cases, that might be true. In most situations, though, it's not. They are women just like you. You might think they had a birthright, being born into middle-class or wealthy families, or one of the 'old names' or the 'squattocracy'. No, and in some cases, it's the absolute opposite. You might think they have had an expensive education in a private school—a couple have, but generally not. You might think they left their region of origin in order to pursue their careers and that they couldn't possibly have succeeded by staying local. In fact, this book is all about the fact that many did stay regional, by choice, and made it work for them as an advantage.

Sandberg said that writing her book was an example of herself 'leaning in'. Likewise, in writing this book I am honouring my commitment to other women in regional areas, and acknowledging their contribution to the nation. I want this book to be read by such women, who look in the mirror and say "I can't". I want them to reframe that to "I'm not ready YET, and I'm working on it", and then to "I CAN and I AM".

The difference I describe in these women's stories, is their belief that it was possible. There are a range of factors that have enabled them to take risks, steer themselves into the right areas, and see possibilities they might otherwise not have pursued.

For the women I've interviewed, other women have helped them along the way, and have provided mentoring, guidance and support.

However, this book might also be helpful for boys and men. While my purpose is in writing for women, and that's my passion, I recognise that there are also young men who lack aspiration or who are not sure what to do with it. There are also fathers who want things to be different for their daughters. A direct Facebook message on my consulting page, from a dad named Mark, sums that up:

> I have four daughters in my family and I am concerned about their treatment as they enter the workforce. If there was a program that worked through the basics for men, this can only improve the future. Good luck with what you do.

I know I can't change the world with one book. I'm realistic. I do know that society is challenged by violence towards women, poor health outcomes for women, and older women in poverty. I do know that if I can write something that inspires women to reach one step higher, and to believe they can, they will be more confident and have a stronger sense of self. This means I can potentially contribute to better women's independence, health, and wellbeing, and I'm happy with that.

....

We don't need more self-help books. We don't need negative self-talk blaming ourselves for not leaning in. Nor do we need more lists of 'ten ways to improve' our career prospects. We need practical, forward-moving actions that we design and own, for which we can hold ourselves accountable.

Enjoy the book, and get your spade ready.

PART 1

THE GRASS CEILING AND WHY WE SHOULD CUT THROUGH

CHAPTER 1

DEFINING THE GRASS CEILING

' ... and I can't stand fences
Don't fence me in ...'

—(Thanks to Cole Porter and Robert Fletcher for their 1934 song.)

For many years I have used the term 'grass ceiling' in conversations with female friends and young women I have mentored. I had always used the term in the context that I was based in Southern regional Victoria—great dairy country because of its temperate climate, good rainfall and ability to grow lots of green grass. The fenced pastures always showed me their natural beauty, yet in other ways they were a reminder that we could be fenced in by our own and others' attitudes and perceptions.

For me, the grass ceiling was a play on words based on the glass ceiling term we have come to know so well. It wasn't just the boundary fences; in my view, women were hitting the glass ceiling in regional areas more often than their city sisters. I would talk about work and leadership opportunities women didn't take or were prevented from taking. I treated the words in a light-hearted way. It wasn't until a woman I mentored told me she thought it was a helpful term—and one she would always remember—that I started to think of it more seriously. I began using it in speeches, in wider conversations, and with people whom I told I might write a book one day. The grass ceiling started to have a deeper meaning for me.

What I didn't know then was that other people had used the term in other contexts. The grass ceiling had been referred to by commentators on women's sport, and how girls were pushing through into new frontiers.[1] Angela Pippos wrote about the extraordinary transformation taking place in Australian sport, where women are breaking through the grass ceiling and competing for a fair go.[2] And it's the name of a conference run by the Victorian Women's Trust[3] in 2017.

My research for this book led me to academic work undertaken in the late 1990s by Margaret Alston. Alston's grass ceiling was a compelling read. A little different to my own context, it was a powerful description of the challenges facing rural women.

When Alston published her book *Breaking through the grass ceiling: Women, power and leadership in agricultural organisations*[4], I wonder if she thought that 16 years later the issues she raised would still be as relevant?

Alston's book drew on extensive interviews conducted in 1997–98 with Australian women engaged in agriculture as leaders, farmers, and bureaucrats, and with chairs of boards developing agricultural policy. The book explored discriminatory treatment of rural women and the requirement for many of them to work what she termed 'quadruple shifts', which included farm work, paid work off-farm, childcare, and housework.

As far back as the Karpin Report in 1997, increasing women's access to decision-making in rural areas was said to be a human rights issue. More critically, the Organisation for Economic Co-operation and Development (OECD) reported that women's participation in the rural economy improved Australia's position and performance.

While a lot has changed, and there are more women working and governing in rural Australia, many still experience frustrations in what they see as a lack of career choice and lifestyle options available to them.

It's no longer the 'elephant in the room'. It is talked about openly, and there are self-help books about how women can enhance their career prospects. Rural women do tell me, though, that they feel all this advice is aimed at women working in the city who have many more choices.

I was inspired to write, in part because of my own education, work and life experiences, and in part due to my observations and conversations with other rural and regional women. My community leadership and volunteer work have also played a part in how I see opportunity.

I'm a supporter of diversity policies in organisations, quotas, and open discussion about gender equity. I also know that these things only go part way to helping individual women act on their ambitions. They are highly important, and yet only part of the solution.

In my view, there are several factors at play, which will be explored in more detail throughout the book. These characteristics are also in evidence throughout the stories from the women I interviewed for the case studies, and in the notes about women I have coached and mentored. These factors are:

- a fixed vs growth mindset
- an external vs internal locus of control
- understanding of own values

- perceptions of choice
- preparedness to be visible.

It occurs to me that if rural women are going to close the Aspiration Gap, they need to know how. It can be difficult to feel ill-equipped and alone. Knowing and understanding their self-talk, and where it keeps them, is empowering. Knowing and naming their biases and fears enables them to react differently, and make new choices.

I want to stimulate women to do something. This is not a 'fix regional women' book—I don't think they are broken. Nor is it a book to fix gender inequity in regional areas—that's not possible with writing alone.

I want women to try just one thing, or a few of the things suggested in the book. Read each chapter, do the exercises, select something that makes sense to try. See if it works. If yes, success, and move on to the next idea. If no, try something else and keep going. Believe. Seek out other women and men who can help you to be bold for change.

For the women I coach and mentor across regional Australia, real change occurs when they open their minds to the options available; when they know their own values system; when they are willing to explore outside the 'small pond'; and, create their own visibility. Possibilities start to arise that they never thought of before.

My passion is seeing women achieving the things to which they aspire. This means getting the jobs they want, meeting the people they want to influence, and having fulfilled lives. I help women flourish in their careers; I help them to envision a broader life so they can attain personal meaning and values alignment. I help them cut through their own grass ceiling so they can step out onto the manicured lawn of their choosing.

CHAPTER 2

CUTTING THROUGH FOR THE WORLD'S ECONOMY

"Women are the most underutilized economic asset in the world's economy."[1]

—Angel Gurría, Secretary-General, OECD

I have previously referred to the cost, to the individual woman, of not cutting through the grass ceiling: the impact of not having financial independence and possible poorer health outcomes. However, there are wider costs to us as a society, and to regional communities.

With global change, widespread international acceptance of the importance of gender equity, and awareness of women's roles in the new economy, the world is changing rapidly. There has never been a better time for regional Australian women to aim for greater success at work, and to make their aspirations possible.

Bernice Ledbetter says:

> Women make up nearly half the workforce in nearly every country around the world ... The urgency for managing the talent for that half of the workforce suggests it is time to ... bring more women into positions of influence and leadership ... this is necessary if

organizations hope to create and sustain economic competitive advantage.[2]

The Gender Pay Gap Report[3] describes an average of 8% difference in pay between men and women across all job roles and sectors. The report states that if you are born today, you will be 80 years old before the gender pay gap is closed. This is a statistic we hear a lot these days. It is thrown around readily. **I'm not sure it's true.**

Many companies today know that women are crucial to the success of the global economy. In 2009, Michael J Silverstein and Kate Sayre said:

> ... women are increasingly gaining influence in the work world. As we write, the number of working women in the United States is about to surpass the number of working men ... To be fair, women are still paid less, on average, than men, and are more likely to work part-time ... Nevertheless, we believe ... women not only will represent one of the largest market opportunities in our lifetimes but also will be an important force in spurring a recovery and generating new prosperity.[4]

Vast reserves of research illustrate that companies with women working in the C-suite can be more profitable. In a US-based study, it was found that going from having no women in corporate leadership to a 30% female share is associated with a one-percentage-point increase in net margin—which translates to a 15% increase in profitability for a typical firm.[5]

Michael McGaughy writes about the increasing number of women in leadership in emerging international markets. He quotes the examples of Korea and Taiwan, which together account for 26% of the MSCI's Emerging Markets Index—both had female presidents from 2016.[6]

In conjunction, female entrepreneurship is the rocket ship of the next decade of growth. Sallie Krawcheck, the CEO and Founder of

Ellevest, writes about women entrepreneurs. She says, '2016 will be the year in which the forces of entrepreneurialism and feminism converge'. [7] Krawcheck, who believes women are driving a surge in start-up businesses globally, finds:

- more systems to support women-owned businesses
- falling costs of technology and cloud-based systems
- diminishing costs of running businesses
- success stories in the mass media that show it can be done
- there is a growing number of older women who are living longer and are more willing to take some risks in the economy.

Another US commentator, Susan Bender-Phelps[8], describes what she calls the Boomer Brain Drain. She says the generational shift occurring right now means there will not be enough men in Generation X to fill the void created by retiring Baby Boomers. Consequently, Bender-Phelps says, 'this is great news for women'.

CHAPTER 3

CUTTING THROUGH FOR THE AUSTRALIAN ECONOMY

'Lest you think that this is all old history and irrelevant to the present day, it is worth recalling that there are women who were in the workforce at the time of the equal pay decisions who are still in the workforce today or only recently retired.'

—Luci Ellis[1]

The National Seniors Australia website[2] shows that our largest population cohort is the 'baby boomer' generation, made up of almost 5.6 million Australians born between 1946 and 1965, who are now leaving the paid workforce—and will continue to do so for the next 20 years.

If regional women are well-prepared for this transition, there will be opportunities to step up into leadership roles, and to work for extended periods for as long as they wish. Career and development opportunities, for mature women, are well documented by Aviva Wittenberg-Cox in *What Work Looks Like for Women in Their 50s.*[3]

Technology is also making an enormous difference to women's participation choices. The global professional services company, Accenture, released research in 2016 showing significant change in many economies as a result of digital technology. The company surveyed approximately 5000 men and women in 31 countries. They examined people's use of technology, access to devices like smartphones, and the frequency with which they use them. The survey findings were then combined with data from the World Bank regarding education enrolment, labour participation rates, and numbers of women in leadership roles.

Accenture concluded that digital fluency is helping women gain employment and attain higher levels of education. The research contends that digital literacy is increasingly important in helping women advance at work, and *assists women access opportunities that have not existed before.* Accenture boldly predict that 'if we can double the pace at which women become frequent users of digital technologies, the workplace could reach gender equality by 2040 in developed nations and by 2060 in developing nations'.[4]

If we view Australia in relation to the rest of the world, our place is firmly in the centre of South-East Asia. Futurist Gihan Perera suggests we might be the Switzerland of this part of the planet.

In his blog, Perera discusses the strategic importance of Australia's positioning in the new world economy.[5] For regional Australian women, then, several future factors become important in helping make good choices about careers.

- Population growth trends in regional cities, as Australia heads to 35–50 million people.

- Baby boomer retirement and Generation X moving to 'lifestyle choice' roles in the next 20 years.

- The ability to work anywhere at any time, with tools that connect us to the rest of the world and the nation.

- Less reliance on the institutions that were formerly significant places of employment, such as the public service.

- Less reliance on government policy to structure the economy for participation.

It is important to recognise the disruption in the way we see ourselves, and plan for our future.

In summary, then, this section stresses the importance of rural and regional women in the labour market internationally, and in Australia. Our future prosperity depends on gender equity and in empowering women to have choices.

PART 2

HOW DO I CUT THROUGH?

CHAPTER 4

AM I UNDER THE GRASS CEILING?

To cut through:
To penetrate or slice through something.
To avoid or bypass something complicated;
circumvent something.
To travel across some region, rather than around it.

—(idioms from the Free Dictionary)

Generally, our social structures in regional areas keep us under the grass ceiling. This is not unique to rural Australia; it's a phenomenon of gender inequity all over the world. But many of us place ourselves under the ceiling, or see ourselves remaining there. In these next chapters, we will explore what keeps women under the ceiling.

Before we talk about cutting through, it might be useful to examine what being underneath the grass ceiling sounds like in our heads. The model below shows the comparison between women who are 'below the line' or under the ceiling, and women who are levelling up to cut through.

Below the grass ceiling	Cutting through
It's not fair; there is gender inequity.	There is inequity around me, and I will encounter that in numerous ways throughout my life. In this moment, what can I do to re-balance the scales in my favour?
There are no jobs right for me.	I wonder if I know about all the jobs that are here or coming up? I wonder who I can ask about that?
The jobs that exist here are short-term.	Can I test if this is the truth? Is it right? What opportunities might a short-term role give me? How could that be of benefit?
There isn't a prospect for promotion.	As above, how can I test if this is true?
I have gone as far as I can go here.	Is this right? How do I know this? If it's true: What does it mean. What, if anything, will I do with that?
I'm invisible to decision-makers; no one sees me.	I can take some clear actions to increase my visibility. I can get advice about how. I can find a mentor to help me.
The better jobs all require me to work a long distance away and for too many hours—I can't have a life.	I know some people who commute and they seem to make it work well. Maybe I can talk to them about how they manage. I can explore different organisational policies for options such as working from home part-time, and virtual meetings, etc.
Women don't get opportunities here or only some women do, but not women like me.	I know a few women who have been promoted here. I can ask them about their experiences and find out more about them. I can ask one to mentor me.
It's not my time, I'm not ready.	What does ready look like? What will I have done to be ready? What is ready enough?
I don't have the qualifications.	I wonder if the qualifications are mandatory? I wonder if my qualifications and experience satisfy that criteria? Who can I talk to about this? How else do I meet the selection requirements? If I were a man, would I have a try anyway?
I'm not a natural leader.	How am I defining leadership? Where else in my life have I displayed leadership? For example, in sports, childhood activities, committees I have chaired. What have I learned from these experiences about my leadership style? How could I get help to enhance my leadership?
I'm returning to work after a long break – I'm out of step and no employer will want me.	I'm curious about what prospects I might find if I start asking people I know.

Do you recognise any of these statements? Do you see yourself in there? I hear all these things from women during coaching and mentoring sessions and in workshops. They are real experiences and frustrations. I have shared many of them myself.

Questions:

- Are you saying anything from the first column to yourself, now? If so, which statement(s)?

- Which statement(s), from the second column, could you adopt straight away?

- Which one(s) might you need some help to move to?

- Are there other statements that could be helpful for you?

Exercise:

List the statements that keep you under the grass ceiling, and the questions that you could be asking yourself to challenge those assumptions.

CHAPTER 5

BUT I'M STUCK NOW!

'Never stop asking yourself what you want to be when you grow up no matter what you have already achieved and regardless of what stage you are at in life, having the ambition to achieve more can be a wonderful, life-affirming force.'

—Rachel Bridge[1]

In this chapter, we will explore a model that describes our perspectives on career progression, and the various steps along the path to being above the grass ceiling.

In my work over the past 30 years, I've met hundreds of women who tell me they don't want to be superwoman—they can't do it all. Some announce secret fears that they may not be cut out for a leadership role, or that they won't be clever/confident/assertive enough to put themselves forward and succeed.

Most women I've met have described their frustration at climbing the career ladder. They still, almost exclusively, think of career progression as upwards, to higher wages, a bigger title, more responsibility and yes, ego too. We are human after all.

I'm throwing a trowel in the ground here: I disagree that career progression has to be those things. In fact, I argue that progression is a dirty word these days. I want to see women change their view on this entirely. I want women to aim for career *soaring* instead. To me, this is less like a ladder (up and down) and more like a climbing wall: you might head sideways to gain a foothold, take a look at what's next, and learn from those new experiences. You gather your thoughts before moving again. You don't have to climb upwards straight away.

In the following model, we can see the value-transfer women can gain by taking certain steps on the platforms towards achievement—moving from Stuck to Soaring.

from stuck to soaring

soaring
feeling fulfilled – at peak

sought
feeling enhanced – valued lifestyle

searching
feeling optimistic – new opportunities

seeing
feeling open – new perceptions

stuck
feeling limited – closed

© Maree McPherson Consulting

STUCK

Some women experience a sense of being Stuck, or limited in their options. They are unable to see opportunities for progression and feel a detrimental impact in their lives overall. They have the qualifications and experience, yet see only barriers to progress. They might be stuck under the grass ceiling for a while, if they can't change this outlook.

SEEING

Opening perceptions about choices helps women move to Seeing. It doubles the value they perceived before. Women on this platform know they have something more to offer and know they have many options from which to choose. It's simply that the range of options is overwhelming, and they are not sure where to start, or what they need to do next. They have a spade but haven't made the first cut in the soil.

SEARCHING

Some women are Searching for new opportunities to progress and are exploring their increased options. They have had some new experiences; they might have acted in higher duties roles or led new projects. They want the next experience, and are looking at where they can pitch themselves. They are more focused on their destination and require support to network with the right people to help them. They are ready for new positioning. They have dug a couple of holes, and are now waiting to see what falls through.

SOUGHT

At the next platform, there is great progression. Women here have enhanced their income and lifestyle. They are Sought and looked for by employers and others to take on new roles, lead change, and help organisations flourish. They are happy with their achievements, yet wondering what comes next. Despite having good jobs and lifestyles, they see barriers to further progression. They know these barriers can be overcome, but are not sure how or are not confident to try. They sometimes say they have lost their *mojo*. They may feel their options are very limited, and stay a long time in their roles by default. They have dug through to the surface and are just above the grass ceiling on the manicured lawn. They have a very strong sense that there's more. Other people sometimes refer to them as *the big fish in the small pond*.

CUTTING THROUGH THE GRASS CEILING

SOARING

Finally, to the women who have a greater sense of fulfillment about work and life. They believe they have made free choices about the path they have taken. They have achieved their aspirations and feel ready to take on whichever new opportunities arise. They take risks and follow gut instincts. They can see some obstacles, yet know how to get around those, and who to ask for help. They feel self-reliant, and trust their own judgement. They are above the grass ceiling entirely. It no longer matters—they are Soaring.

Questions:

- Where would you place yourself on the ladder?
- Where do you want to be in a year?
- What two things might help you get there?

Exercise:

Imagine you are Soaring. Write down the time-frame you see, and the changes that have taken place in your life to this point. What is this story telling you about any changes you aspire to make?

Time-frame	Changes that have been made

CHAPTER 6

WILL UNCONSCIOUS BIAS KEEP ME UNDER THE GRASS CEILING?

'But I think that no matter how smart, people usually see what they're already looking for, that's all.'

—Veronica Roth, Author

By now, you may be thinking you would love to be Soaring, but the world is so full of gender bias that you can never be where you would like to be. In this chapter, we will examine how *our own* unconscious bias might keep us under the grass ceiling. We will go a step deeper, and describe the *Reticular Activating System* (RAS) before looking at how these two concepts are related.

Let's start with defining unconscious bias. Unconscious bias, sometimes called implicit bias, is a bias of which we are unaware. It may happen outside of our own control. It happens automatically, and we all have several biases of which we are unconscious. In the late 1990s, psychologists Mahzarin Banaji and Anthony Greenwald explored these hidden (unconscious) biases we all carry from our lifetimes of experience. These can be from our traditional attitudes about age, gender, race, ethnicity, sexuality, disability and other factors. Banaji and Greenwald used the Implicit Association Test to establish the hidden biases of their subjects. They wrote about their revolutionary findings in their book, *Blindspot*.[1]

We spend a lot of our time in our minds, creating our own future pictures. In this process, we bring forth thoughts, feelings, beliefs, values, dreams and memories of previous actions. We do this irrespective of our conscious awareness. Our RAS is located in the core of our brain stem. The RAS takes its instructions from our conscious mind and passes them on to our subconscious mind. As a consequence of this biological function, whatever we are focusing on will percolate through to our subconscious mind. It will then appear at a future time.

For example, have you ever had a desire to eat hot chips? From that moment, everywhere you look, people all around you are eating hot chips. You've never seen so many chips! That is how the RAS works. It's seeing the things you're looking for subconsciously.

I first heard about the RAS from one of my mentors, Donna McGeorge, at a facilitation training workshop. It immediately got me thinking about the connection to our unconscious biases about ourselves. I have worked with many women who reinforce their views of themselves unconsciously, by continually keeping their RAS programmed for that very same perspective.

MEET JESS

Jess was a young woman I met for some mentoring sessions. She was looking to better position herself for future promotion at work. She loved her job and commuted every day for several hours. I recall saying, "That sounds so hard. I wonder how you keep from being overtired".

(I had to laugh at myself. I'm a coach who specialises in helping people stretch themselves and to love their jobs, yet I immediately assumed that her commute was dragging Jess down. Shameful of me.)

Her response was, "Well, of course I wouldn't do it for just any employer. This is a great company, and I love my job, so it doesn't feel like work. I know what I'm doing, and there's plenty more to learn. It's easy to stay motivated."

It was clear to me, as we talked, that there were some good reasons why Jess liked her job so much.

- *Her values aligned with those of her employers. She felt they cared for her. They proved this by offering flexible working opportunities, accommodation and transport home if needed.*

- *She was well positioned to develop her career. She could see where her role fitted within the goals of the team.*

- *Her manager offered her useful feedback about her good work. He also told her where she can learn from misjudgements.*

- *She felt she was well paid.*

I would add a further factor; that Jess could see these positives because she tuned her RAS to look for them. As a consequence, she felt in control. It's her choice to work in the job. That made all the difference to her mindset about work.

Much has been written about the very real impact of unconscious gender bias in holding women back in work and society. Lisa Marie Jenkins described it this way:

> There is a silent, yet powerful force - unconscious gender bias and we all have it, men and women. Even if you are pro-women, this bias looms unconsciously, unless conscious action is taken to shift your default mode of thinking. There is actually a neuroscience behind it.[2]

But what if some of that unconscious bias is our own? How often do we self-impose barriers to our success, without even knowing we do so? Very often, the bias we are facing is our own. We need to own it and get it out of the way. Our own unconscious bias very likely gets in our way.

Let's face it, the majority of women with whom you speak every day will say their success came from hard work, sheer luck, or help from other people. We simply won't acknowledge it is our own intellect, political nous, reading of a situation, or innate intuition that explains our success. Nathalie Salles describes situations where women undermine themselves without realising their behaviour is affecting their progress.[3] Carol Sankar writes about the Belief Gap, she says, " ... our fear of rejection will inevitably hold us back from taking a risk if everything is not 'perfect'".[4]

Nathalie Gevinti declares that women are 'creatures of habit' who like 'clinging to certainty and to what we consider our identity. Even when we don't like that identity'.[5] Gevinti says that by constantly looking at what doesn't work in society (i.e. the glass ceiling) we keep reinforcing that idea. In contrast, she quotes many successful women who have made it to where they aspired.

What these authors are referring to is a type of unconscious bias we hold for ourselves, and its relationship to seeing only what we look for. Our ability to create our own future relates to the part of our brain that serves as the filter between our conscious and subconscious minds.

Questions:

- What biases do you hold against yourself?

- How is your RAS holding you back? What are you looking for that you always see?

- How are you clinging to parts of your identity that you don't like?

Exercise:

Write three statements you can repeat to yourself that will reset your RAS to see positive resources or role models.

Statement 1	
Statement 2	
Statement 3	

CHAPTER 7

COMPARISONS CAN KEEP US UNDER THE GRASS CEILING

I'd like to make a note about comparisons here. Comparisons are easy to make, yet they don't always serve us. Comparisons can be our enemy or our friend. We often compare ourselves with other women. This is very often counter-productive and can make us feel inadequate.

The stories at the end of this book are designed to give you insights into the challenges and highlights experienced by other women at various stages in their careers and lives. The women I have interviewed want you to gain strength and empowerment from their examples, not to compare and undermine yourself.

When we compare, we are usually not comparing apples with apples, but rather oranges, lemons, and many other fruits. We simply don't have all the facts, and can't possibly know what else is occurring for people. However, we CAN use their stories and experiences to 'ground truth' our own understanding and to set goals for ourselves.

Leon Festinger developed social comparison theory in 1954.[1] This theory is a good way to explain the comparisons we make between others and ourselves.

When we are comparing negatively, we find ourselves seeking perfection—this is an illusion. We tell ourselves life isn't fair. We can turn our friends into rivals in our own minds. We can behave destructively. When we are comparing positively, on the other hand, we can use our comparisons to set goals, and troubleshoot.

I am a member of a business school called Thought Leaders. One of the elements of the Thought Leaders Business School is that we have a belt system, a bit like martial arts, to describe the revenue in our businesses. There are White Belts through to Black Belts, with White being the lowest revenue per annum and Black being the highest, and so on through several Dans. For those in the lower Belt levels, it is very easy to compare with the people running Black Belt revenue streams.

We can make a choice. We can choose to be negative and focus on all the lucky breaks they might have had (usually imaginary!), that they started out with more than we did, that they've had more help, they are cleverer, they know more people, etc. Or we can choose to learn from their experience, hear their stories, take up the advice they give us, and model on the behaviours and strategies that have been successful for them, all the while setting ourselves immediate, medium, and longer-term goals to work towards.

Please choose to use the stories generously provided by the women who follow later in the book, with a growth mindset and for positive comparison.

CHAPTER 8

CUTTING THROUGH FEAR AND RISK

'Everything you've ever wanted is on the other side of fear.'

—George Addair

Fear is a strange feeling. It's an adrenalin rush, caused by a significant emotion that can grip us for a short time, or it can be slow-burning and long-lasting. This is often related to a lack of confidence and an aversion to risk.

Women can be risk averse in their careers. For regional women, this may play out slightly differently. Regional women might aspire to a certain level and be content to be 'a big fish in a small pond'. However, having the courage to undertake a diverse range of career experiences in different locations, and outside of societal 'norms', can lead to valuable career and life-making opportunities. This can mean making choices to do things differently. It might mean stepping 'sideways', changing industry sectors, working away from home, joining a larger organisation at another level, and so on.

In fact, swimming out of the pond might mean you are a smaller fish for a while, but you get to float in some incredible places. Author and journalist, Malcolm Gladwell, talks about the way in which we sometimes define ourselves based on our peer group.

In an interview for Inc.Video[1] he describes how small ponds can be very helpful spaces. Although he was referring to start-ups and new ventures, I feel his view is also useful for career women. There is no doubt that jumping straight into a highly competitive field before you are quite ready can have a lasting impact, and keep fear as a blocker for way too long.

To me, 'pond life' is interesting on many levels. The women featured in this book reveal that their enhanced experiences led to better careers, lives that are more satisfying, and broader horizons. They prove the recipe for success in swimming out—surviving and thriving.

After many years' experience working with regional and rural people—leading and coaching—I conclude that women, in particular, often have a fear that keeps them from acting on their career goals. To my mind, this is based on where they place the *locus of control* for their lives, and how fixed their *mindset* is. Let's explore those two elements.

MINDSET

Carol Dweck is a Professor of Psychology at Stanford University in the United States of America. Her primary work has been on the psychological trait of mindset, and the difference between those individuals who have a fixed versus a growth mindset. In her groundbreaking book[2], Dweck explains that people with a 'fixed mindset' see their intelligence, capabilities and talents as fixed and unchangeable. These people tend to say, "I can't do that" or "I'm not good at that". Whereas people with a 'growth mindset' believe they can develop themselves further, and are ready for new opportunities. They see challenges as exciting and inspiring. These are the people who know they are outside their comfort zone and look at what they can learn from that experience. People with a growth mindset tend to say, "I can't do that ... *yet*".

Dweck's frameworks are based on praising perseverance, or grit, and resilience, rather than talent. Her work is now internationally recognised in education systems, and is influencing the way learning occurs in Australian schools. *It is also influencing the way we think about career progression.*

LOCUS OF CONTROL

In the 1950s, Julian Rotter[3] developed a theory about how much control people believed they had over their own life circumstances. He concluded that people with an external 'locus of control' often blame external influences for the things that happen to them, and that those with an internal locus of control believed they could influence events and outcomes for themselves. The underlying question within this theory is whether we control our own lives, or whether external forces determine them.

What happens when mindset and locus of control combine?

In my experience, mindset and locus of control are two very powerful contributors to the fear that holds women back in their careers. If women can master these two psychological forces, they can take steps towards achieving their goals. Let's look at the several aspects where the two psychological theories connect.

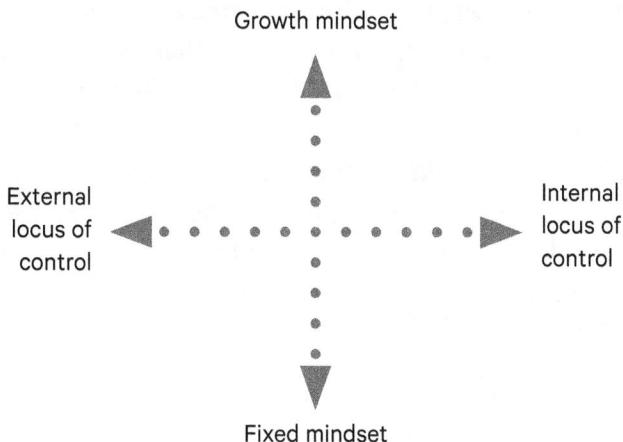

Growth mindset

External locus of control ← → Internal locus of control

Fixed mindset

43

Fixed mindset: external locus

Remember the days when you got into the toddler pool only? You could stand up. The water wasn't too deep for you, and it felt safe. It was easy to get out if you chose.

When our locus of control is external and our mindset is fixed, we are fearful of swimming outside the small pond. We fear three main things: loss, failure and *success*. It's easier to stay in the toddler pool where we are safe, where we won't have to give up our place or status; we won't drown, and we won't be a superstar or draw attention to our talents. We maintain the view that what we have is all we *can* have. Our attributes will remain throughout life. In the earlier chapter, *Am I under the grass ceiling?* many of the statements on the left side of the table belong with a fixed mindset and external locus. The statements focus on societal factors or other people for our status. They show a lack of belief that things can change, and that WE can change.

Fixed mindset: internal locus

Some of us might place ourselves on the reserve swim team. We don't think we are ready for the A-team, and it's simply too much of a risk to step forward. We know we can swim already, but our fixed mindset has us thinking we won't improve our stroke or become any faster. Due to our internal locus, we know we can take responsibility for our own choices, but that brings risks. There are three risks for us. The risk of rejection by others if we put ourselves forward—they might not want us on the team. The risk of reputation—we could be exposed as a fraud, and not having the talents we said we had. Finally, there's the risk of regret—it's too hard to consider that in the future we might be kicking ourselves that we didn't take the opportunity to be on the A-team when it was presented to us.

In February 2017, Raina Brands and Isabel Fernandez-Matteo[4] published an article about a study they had conducted with more than 10,000 senior executives competing for management roles in the United Kingdom. They found that:

> ... women were indeed less likely than men to apply for these jobs, but ... we found that women were much less likely to apply for a job if they had been rejected for a similar job in the past. Of course, men were also less likely to apply if they had been rejected, but the effect was much stronger for women — more than 1.5 times as strong.

Brands and Fernandez-Matteo concluded that women take themselves out of competition as a natural consequence of being in a 'negatively stereotyped minority' where they have 'concerns that they would not be valued or truly accepted at the highest levels in the organization'. In their view, ' ... women tend to place greater weight than men do on the fairness of the recruitment and selection processes. This is because fair treatment is interpreted by female managers as a signal that they belong and are accepted'.

Growth mindset: external locus

Many of us start with a growth mindset, and this serves us well. However, when combined with an external locus of control, we can still hold ourselves back. We are brave enough to put ourselves in the deep end of the Olympic pool. We do swim outside our traditional boundaries. We know we can learn to float, tread water and swim back to the shallow end when we need to. We become curious about what we can do to develop further.

Our curiosity peaks in three areas: how much more can we learn, how much capacity for change we have, and what options might emerge for us?

Growth mindset: internal locus

Finally, we become captain of the swim team. It's possibly been a long haul, and hard work. We have trained at early hours, have spent time supporting and energising others, and have taken heed of the advice of our coaches and mentors. We have allowed ourselves to grow and improve our stroke so that we are faster and have more stamina and resilience in the pool. We are self-driven as much as others encourage us. Despite external factors, which might work against us, we have taken a risk and put our hand up to be captain anyway. Who cares if we don't get it? We won't know if we don't try. We're ready, and if it doesn't happen this round, it WILL happen next time, or in another club or team. When women have a growth mindset and an internal locus of control, we leap out of the small pond and start swimming wherever we like. We simply keep swimming and exploring along the way. This is where women start to see real value in their careers. It's a time when referrals, offers and promotions become apparent.

MEET LESLEY

When I met Lesley, she was on the verge of something great. She felt it, and she knew she could influence what would occur next. Lesley had decided it was the right time in her life to start swimming beyond the small pond. Her children were both at school, and her partner was supportive of her making changes in her career. She applied for a place in a regional leadership program so that she could explore her capacity, learn and grow in a community of others, and network with people from new sectors she hadn't connected to previously. It also took her beyond the boundaries of the small town where she lived and worked. The next time I saw Lesley was four months later. What she told me showed she had allowed a growth mindset to influence her thinking, and an internal locus of control to spur action. As a consequence of positioning herself among others and putting her hand up, Lesley had been offered something new and exciting. She had stepped into what others might call a 'sideways' role which allowed her to complete a distinct and new project. Such was the value and uniqueness of her work that a major university approached her to undertake a doctorate in the field, and they connected her to an international organisation associated with the work. Lesley was becoming the 'go to' person on the regional aspects of her work, not just for Australia, but for the Western world. Dr Lesley was just over the horizon (... ok, with a lot of hard work and some tears I'll assume, we know PhDs aren't a walk in the park).

The interesting thing about Lesley's story is that the sideways move positioned her so well. Lesley said she thought that move might have been damaging for her, yet she decided to take it anyway, and see what she could draw from it. It was a role that other women might have viewed as "my boss just wants me out of the way, I'm becoming a threat."

What's also interesting is that Lesley did this despite a lack of encouragement and understanding from some of the people who matter most to her, including close friends and her family. Lesley described them as loving people who gave her good support in many ways, but they simply didn't understand or value her desire to do more, or explore the world outside their town. She knew they would say things that might hurt (unintentionally or otherwise), and would question her judgement, her view of herself (so you think you're better than us do you? A PhD!?) and her commitment to her partner and children. Because of her internal locus of control, Lesley knew she could step beyond this. Because of her growth mindset, she knew she could keep learning and developing, and she allowed her friends and family to have the opportunity to grow too, by her example.

Questions:

- Do you have a fixed or a growth mindset?

- List two statements you can say to yourself when trying something new, that will help you maintain a growth mindset.

- Do you generally have an external or internal locus of control?

- In what ways could you shift your locus of control thinking?

Exercise:

You can complete the Locus of Control questionnaire (22 questions) for your own interest via the Mindtools website https://www.mindtools.com/pages/article/newCDV_90.htm

CHAPTER 9

FROM FEAR AND RISK TOWARDS CURIOSITY AND BOLDNESS

In this chapter, we are opening the elements that either block us or free us to take action. We will consider fear, risk, curiosity and boldness, and how these manifest in our lives.

FEAR

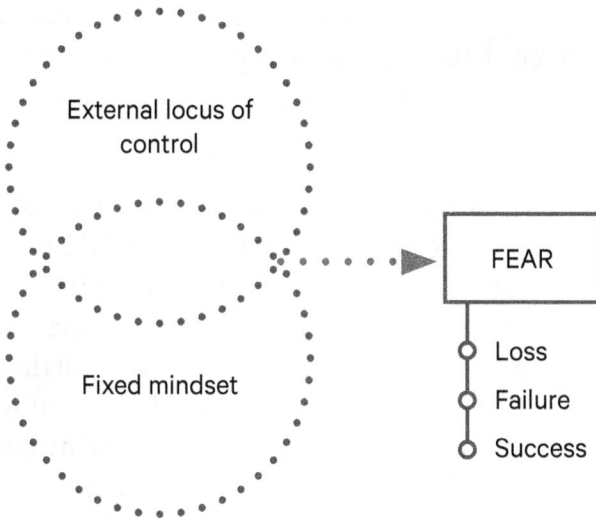

Fear is an emotion that can block us from acting for extended periods. Fear can take three forms in how it impacts our career decisions. We can experience fear of loss, fear of failure, and fear of success.

Fear of loss

When we are afraid of losing something important to us, we might not act on an opportunity. We are afraid that choosing to act means giving something up. Fear of loss holds us back from taking up our choices. This fear can be like getting a new pet. A friend of mine was so saddened by the death of his dog, that when his partner suggested getting another one, he refused. He knew that one day he would have to deal with another dog's death. He decided not to have a dog at all, because his grief would be too much. His fear of loss blocked him from experiencing the joy and love of a new dog in his life.

Daniel Kahneman, along with his colleague, Amos Tversky, developed another psychological theory, prospect theory[1] in the late 1970s. Through this work, they concluded that people experience 'loss aversion'. They defined this as people having a tendency to prefer avoiding loss rather than acquiring gain. Later studies have suggested that losses may even be twice as psychologically powerful as gains.

When I was offered a new job in Melbourne, I had to face some powerful fears of my own. The job meant I would be relocating weekdays and living apart from my husband. It was an initial three-year contract and the prospect of living apart for that many years almost led me to decline the job offer. I thought of all the negatives and the things I would miss. It was my husband who helped me to list the positives, and all the things I would gain by making that move. He also helped me see how we could make it work for our relationship. It remains one of the best choices I made in my life, and I stayed in that role for more than my initial three years.

Fear of failure

Sometimes we say 'no' to opportunities because we are afraid of failure. Fear of failure can be a paralysis that stops us from acting. Remember exam time at school? Remember your weakest subject? Can you recall what it felt like to be afraid to fail that subject, or to fail that class based on your results through the year? That fear of failure made many students throw away their books and give up. "I'll only fail this subject anyway, so there's no point studying for the exam."

MEET JULIANNE

Julianne's manager wanted her to take a promotion to team leader—he saw her potential and could see she was bored and under-stimulated, and that it was affecting her behaviour. He knew she described 'hating' her job to a couple of trusted colleagues. He also knew she was so afraid of failing that he couldn't convince her to change roles. He wasn't sure why. He referred Julianne to me.

When Julianne came for coaching, we dealt with the immediate presenting issues she faced at work. After a few sessions, she revealed her deepest career fears, and why she thought she might be holding herself back. At key points in her life— primary and secondary school, and in her first job—she had been disciplined harshly for failing at things. She had not been able to develop the perseverance and growth mindset required for her to trust new tasks and changing situations. Her view was "I'll be no good at the team leader job. I'll just disappoint my boss and my team". Julianne came to see how negatively this was affecting her life overall, and how to work on turning that around.

Fear of failure can get in our way and stunt our growth. It can stop us making the best choices for our lives. It can stop us from knowing joy.

Dr. Brené Brown, Research Professor at the University of Houston Graduate College of Social Work, sums up this conundrum beautifully when she says, "When I'm standing at the crossroads of fear and gratitude, I've learned that I must choose vulnerability and practice gratitude if want to know joy."[2]

Fear of success

Fear of success can also stop action. We sometimes stall our careers because we are fearful of what success might mean. Many of us remember the feeling of being teased or bullied at school for doing well. Whether this was academically, or on the sporting field or in creative arts, we might have been the 'teacher's pet' or the 'tall poppy'. Sometimes, we almost resent having the talents or achievements that others desire.

Some writers recognise this fear as the Jonah complex.[3] Often credited to Abraham Maslow, or his colleague. Frank Manuel, the Jonah complex is the fear of success which prevents us reaching our full potential. It can mean that we avoid our destiny and keep ourselves smaller.

For women, this fear can relate to the potential impacts of success. It might mean not being liked, damaging relationships with loved ones and friends, being criticised as undeserving of achievements, or gaining more responsibility.

It not only stops action, it can create self-sabotage. We have all seen examples of women who have closed social media accounts because of 'online trolling'. Their success has affected others in such a way that it can erupt into public criticism and derision, and sometimes threats. Yet, it doesn't have to be so dramatic to stop us from making change.

I had an exchange with a woman who attended one of my workshops. She said she had almost decided not to attend after enrolling, because she couldn't access her usual childcare. She had to take her son to her mother's home for the day. When I asked her why that was something that might have stopped her attending she said, "Well, I couldn't tell my mum I was doing a women's career workshop. I told her I was doing some computer training." I must have looked suitably perplexed, and she went on to explain, "Oh, my mum would have thought I was getting way above myself if I'd said what your workshop was about. She would think that was really snooty. I've never told her what my career means to me or what my goals are. She just doesn't get it. I've actually made decisions to not apply for jobs based on what my parents would say if I got the job". I'm very glad she attended the workshop and focused on changing this self-sabotaging behaviour.

RISK

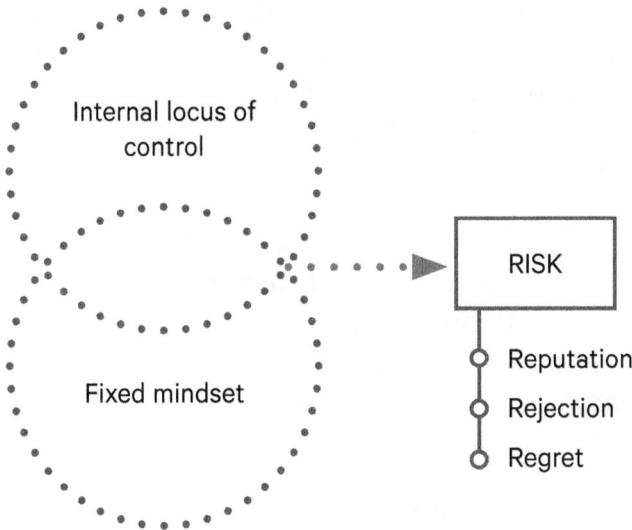

Some of us prefer to stay in the small pond because we are afraid of risk. To my mind, there are three major elements of risk that affect our behaviour and stop us acting. These are the risk to our reputation, the risk of being rejected and the risk we might have regrets.

Risk to reputation

This element of risk is strongly aligned with fear of failure and fear of success. At times, we miss opportunities because we are concerned about how we might look. This can include people's view that we have an over-inflated ego, or that our strong personal image might be damaged by taking an opportunity and not making a good fist of it.

When I was at high school, we often had 'casual clothes' days as special events. These were days when the entire student population could come dressed in their own choice of clothes. Some students loved the freedom of choice this allowed. I hated it. I was so obsessed with what people would think of the things I wore. I was quite a bohemian teen and didn't really stick to the latest fashions. While I loved my clothes and they looked great to me, some other girls would judge me as out of step. It took me some years to learn that finding my own style would be a significant strength for me, and would become a part of my professional reputation. It didn't feel like that at high school.

Personal brand management has become so important in our society that we are all urged to seek help to make sure our careers flourish on our reputation. Personal branding authority Jane Anderson says that, on its own, "hard work doesn't cut it anymore". Anderson's book, *Impact*,[4] is built around her specialisation in helping people create their best image.

Our need for a strong reputation in our careers means we might stop ourselves from pursuing a goal if we see it as risking how we are perceived. This can be especially so if we think that an opportunity isn't one that other people would view as positively as we do. Several of my clients tell me they see risk in what they perceive as a 'sideways step' in their career, not an upwards one. One woman said to me very recently,

> I took a sideways step to go to my current job. Right now, I have another great offer, which I'd be very happy to take ... but I just can't. It's another sideways move at the same level, and people will think I don't want to progress upwards.

She would rather have missed out on the offer on the table, one that she knew would create happiness and excitement for her, because of the way she believed other people in the organisation would view her, and what that might mean for her reputation.

Risk of rejection

Just like feeling fear of failure, we can also be conscious of the risk of rejection. I've met many women who decide not to put themselves forward for opportunities because they might not be chosen. "I can't apply for that job: what if I don't get it?" I have heard women say this many times. Just like the line-up on the sports field where teams are being chosen, we risk being the last girl chosen for a side and we can recall the feeling of not being popular or liked. Of course, being chosen last for softball might have nothing to do with being liked. It might have been a very practical decision on the part of the two captains because you were pretty ordinary at softball— maybe you were always chosen first for a different game or activity.

Just like the school sports field, we might not be the right fit for a job or have the exact skills, or, although we are a strong candidate, there might simply be someone even better. The fact is we will never know this until we try. We need to overcome the risk of rejection.

As Margie Warrell so eloquently puts it,

> Unless you're made of psychological Teflon, it's hard not to feel the sting of being rejected. Yet many people cut themselves off from the possibility of getting what they want because of their fear of how they'll feel if they are rejected in the process. Put another way: **We reject ourselves before anyone else has a chance to do it!**[5]

Risk of regret

Philosopher, Ruth Chang, makes powerful points about decisions and how difficult they can be[6]. One of the most difficult aspects when making a choice is the risk we might feel regretful afterwards. What if we regret the decision we have made?

At one of my women's workshops, a participant spoke of the regret she felt at not having taken a new role she had been offered. It was in another branch of her company, which meant a longer commute and longer hours for her children in childcare. She anticipated the hardship of those two things. Underneath that, though, she acknowledged the fear of being successful in the new role and what that might bring. So she stayed in her role. She held this position for a long time; she liked her colleagues but the job had lost its challenge. To quote her, "Work for me now is like watching a boring movie. I'm biding my time each day until it's over and knowing these are hours of my life I will never get back."

Regret theory suggests that we anticipate regret when we make choices that are uncertain. Loomes and Sugden[7] found that when making choices, we try to mitigate against future regret. When we can't do so, we self-criticise by thinking we should have been able to predict that we would have regrets. I believe that this way of thinking prevents some of us from acting when opportunities are available to us.

Perhaps the most useful way to reframe our thinking is to flip it from risk of regret to curiosity to learn. We are going to unpack this concept in the next section.

CURIOSITY

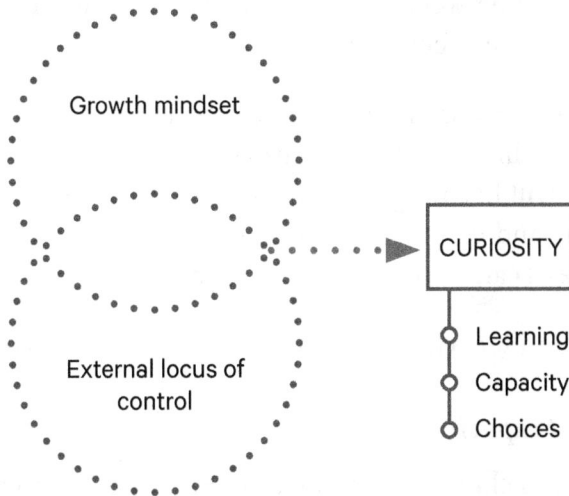

Curiosity didn't kill Ms Cat. As we all know, Ms Cat has nine lives, and on one of her subsequent tries, she got the cream. The point I am making here is that developing a curious mindset will help us achieve our career goals. Curiosity enables us to start asking questions of ourselves and others. Questions like, 'I wonder what I would do if I backed myself?' Women who allow themselves to be curious are interested in three aspects of their careers. What they might learn, what capacity they have for development, and what options are available. Let's explore the three elements of curiosity.

Curious to learn

When we are curious about learning, we open ourselves to new information and ideas. Asking yourself what would happen if you did something new, asked a different question, or applied new information, can be highly enlightening.

According to Jeff Boss, "curiosity fuels competence." Boss puts forward the idea that we have a knowledge gap between our current state and our future state. He says, "to be curious is to have a knowledge gap between what you currently know and what you need to know to be effective".[8]

I believe we learn more when we are curious and open to information. It's like doing a science experiment. You wonder what the outcome will be. You have a hypothesis. You test the facts by being curious and experimenting. It helps you find out whether your hypothesis can be proven.

Stay curious and see what types of learning open up to you.

Curious about capacity

Ms Cat learns to climb trees as a kitten. She learns from watching other cats and mimicking their behaviours. She learns what works to get her up the tree and what doesn't—quickly! She might however try new routes on her climb. She is curious about what she can do.

Curiosity helps us understand what we are capable of. We can enhance our capacity and skills by comprehending what they are, and knowing the gaps we must close. Noel Burch developed his model of the Four Stages of Learning[9] when he was employed at Gordon Training International. Burch wanted to understand people's capacity for learning in more depth. The model suggests that we start out unaware of how little we know, or that we are unconscious of our incompetence. As we start to recognise our incompetence, we consciously take up a new skill, then we consciously employ it. Over time, we can use that skill without thinking about it. At that point, we are said to have reached the point of unconscious competence.

MEET GEENA

Geena wanted to develop her communication skills and came to me for assistance. She knew, based on performance feedback and from comments made by her colleagues (including non-verbal cues), that she had a slightly aggressive communication style. She knew this was blocking her career progress, and it was making life uncomfortable at the office.

Geena was curious about her capacity to understand herself and to learn some new techniques. Over several sessions, Geena practiced some communication methods with me. She read materials I gave to her, and others she researched for herself. She kept a journal about how her communication with others at work and at home progressed. She did this so she could be mindful of what she was learning, and so she could notice particular strategies that worked best for her. Over time, Geena developed an unconscious competence about her communication. It came to her naturally.

Curious about choices

When we have a curious mindset, we can see more choices. Curiosity provokes new thinking and questions. This leads us to explore options we might otherwise have ignored or avoided. Asking ourselves questions such as, 'I wonder what it would be like to try that?' and 'I wonder how I could make that work?' means we can consider different choices.

Jaclyn was facing redundancy from her job. She approached coaching with a curious mindset and wanted to find out what kinds of choices she could make for her next career step. Jaclyn had worked in one sector for a long time—almost 25 years. She had a lot of experience and skills she could transfer to other industries. She also had wisdom and knowledge she could hire out to other organisations on a contract or project basis.

Jaclyn found herself thinking about multiple types of work, or the option of consulting. She had never considered these things before. What had seemed like a closing door suddenly appeared to be many open doors along a corridor. She spent some time in coaching opening each door to look at her choices. She then decided on a course of action.

BOLDNESS

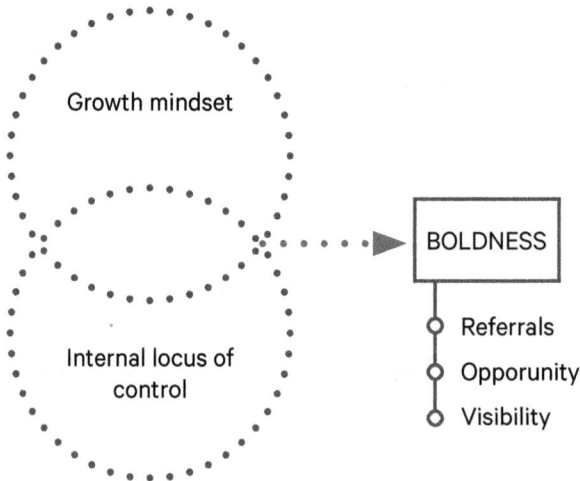

When women are considering swimming in a bigger pond, they need to be bold. In fact, the International Women's Day 2017

hashtag captured this beautifully. *#BeBoldForChange2017*[10] said it all. Stepping up and being bold to make change occur is important—not just for a world that embraces gender equity, but for each of us as individuals. Boldness helps create greater value. Different types of value increase can occur. New referrals and networks, job promotions and opportunities, and often, increased income. I think there are three main areas in which to be bolder. Below, I'm going to detail each of them.

Being Bold – Referrals

Managing referral requires us to be bold. We need to be bold in asking other people to refer us to opportunities. We need to be bold in accepting referrals that are offered. We can maximise this even further by being bold, and making referrals for other women.

Accepting referrals for opportunities can be difficult for many of us. It's a little bit like accepting a compliment. We generally find it harder to accept a compliment than to give one to someone else. It can make us squirm.

However, if we are going to open ourselves to new choices in our careers, we need to be ready to accept such approaches. If a person says she has referred your name to a recruiter with regards to a job opportunity, be bold, say thank you and pursue the call to find out more.

If you are keen to work in an industry or location that you don't know lots about, look for someone you know, or could meet, that can help you. Ask for help. Mentors are out there (and we will read more about them later). There are lots of people willing to help you progress. Be bold and ask.

Finally, be bold and pay it forward. When you refer opportunities to other women or recommend them to others, you are doing two things. You are making them look good and you are making yourself look good. It's not entirely altruistic. You will be viewed more positively if you make recommendations based on your own knowledge, experience and trust of that woman.

As one of my mentoring clients said to me recently.

> I am thankful for the time you have given me as my mentor. I've got a lot from it. It's now my turn to put that information and advice to good use. I'm taking some steps to change my career. I'm also going to mentor another woman in my workplace who is less experienced than me and asking for my help.

Being Bold – Opportunity

I played netball for over 20 years. I played in several different positions, depending on my height at the time. As a tall child, I played goal shooter. As I matured and everyone grew around me, I moved to playing centre because I was smaller and fast. I learned to take opportunities all over the court, and to sneak the ball away from the opposition whenever there was an opening. I had to be very bold at times.

We must be bold to grab opportunities when they arise. Opportunities come in a range of forms: those we seek for ourselves; those others present to us; and those we give to other women, just like referrals.

In her blog for *The Huffington Post*, Evie Hantzopoulos wrote about then US First Lady, Michelle Obama's visit to *Global Kids* headquarters. She describes boldness well, 'The question on everyone's lips was 'How did you get Michelle Obama to visit your program?' The answer is simple: 'One of our students asked'.[11]

When the tap on the shoulder comes your way, be bold and find out more about it. Apply for that job you saw in the newspaper or on line. You can't win a job in which you don't express interest. If an opportunity is promoted to you and you feel it's not right for you at the time, think about a couple of other people it might suit, and mention it to them.

A recruiter I know well, told me that she admires women who take the time to refer others. She says she remembers the women who are honest about a role that isn't right for them, but they have a handful of names of people they know well enough to mention as prospects. They take the time to find out enough details about the job to think it over and decide.

> They are really professional and honest about their needs and aspirations, and are willing to give me a 'heads up' about people who might be a good fit. It really impresses me, and I keep them on my list for the future. They seem to know themselves well, and that's attractive to a recruiter.

Being Bold – Visibility

Of course, none of the former two strategies work if you are invisible. Women who are bold keep themselves visible. Like in a game of hide-and-seek: when dinner is on the table, you want to be found, fast.

The Forbes.com article *Get Visible: The Secrets of Self-Promotion* emphasises the following point, 'Women, ... are likelier to feel that hard work alone is the key to the top—and that means we often underestimate the value of being visible and well-connected in an organization.'[12]

Being bold with your visibility means swallowing your fear and being bold with your profile. My client, Sally, is a good case in point.

MEET SALLY

Sally came to me for coaching when she was leaving her job. She had a few months left of her contract, but she was unsure how much longer she wanted to stay, or how to go about finding her next role. Through her coaching sessions, Sally identified that she wanted to be bolder about her positioning and image. She sought some help to write her professional narrative. She did a short course on maximising her LinkedIn profile, and redeveloped it. She had some professional photos taken. She took the opportunity to look like the people in the jobs she was seeking. She boldly prepared to be her future self.

Being bold about your visibility also requires you to network. Many women say they HATE networking. Yet it's one of the most important things for us to do to boost our careers. Women's networks exist in many areas these days. In the region where I live, for example, there are at least four. Groups like Latrobe Women in Business exist, to ' ... create opportunities where women can come together to think, act, grow and prosper ... Regular events held throughout the year cover topics related to leadership, personal development, finance, business tips and more ... '[13]

Your mentors and colleagues can help you network if it's something you loathe. Be bold and accept invitations to events that will help you meet new people and learn new information. If you are nervous, ask a colleague to join you, and take them as your guest. You will both benefit, and at least you will know one other person. Professional associations are also a great source of networking events. Become a member of a professional body in your area of work. The more people you get to know and can introduce yourself to, the larger your network, and the more you can pay it forward for other women too.

This is your 'boldness toolkit' for taking up change. Like a girl guide, it's important to 'be prepared'.

It's time to reflect on what the elements of fear, risk, curiosity and boldness mean for you.

Questions:

- With which part of the model do you most identify?

- Are you held back by fear and risk, or do you focus more being curious and creating value?

Exercise:

- Identify two ways you could use curiosity to open yourself to new thinking.

- Write down two ways you could be bold, and how you could use that to help meet your career goals.

Ways to be more curious	
1.	2.
Ways to be bolder	
1.	2.
Ways this will help me meet my career goals	
1.	2.

CHAPTER 10

DEVELOPING A POSSIBILITY MINDSET

'Once your mindset changes, everything on
the outside will change along with it.'

—Steve Maraboli, *Life, the Truth, and Being Free*

Women with a Possibility Mindset can find multiple paths of
their own choosing and blending to achieve their desired careers.
Women's possibilities of success are enhanced by being **assertive,
aware, and astute.** Women can move forward from simply seeing
options, through to searching for the right fit and then being
sought-after in their careers.

The Possibility Model above shows the combination of factors that
create a pathway to new possibilities for women. The 'Possibility'
framework I use helps women explore:

- how assertively they are positioning for the future.
- how aware and open-minded they are to opportunities for
  growth and change.
- how astute they are at seeing the choices available to them.

Being visible

Assertive

P

Astute

Aware

Seeing choices

Open minded

P = Possibility

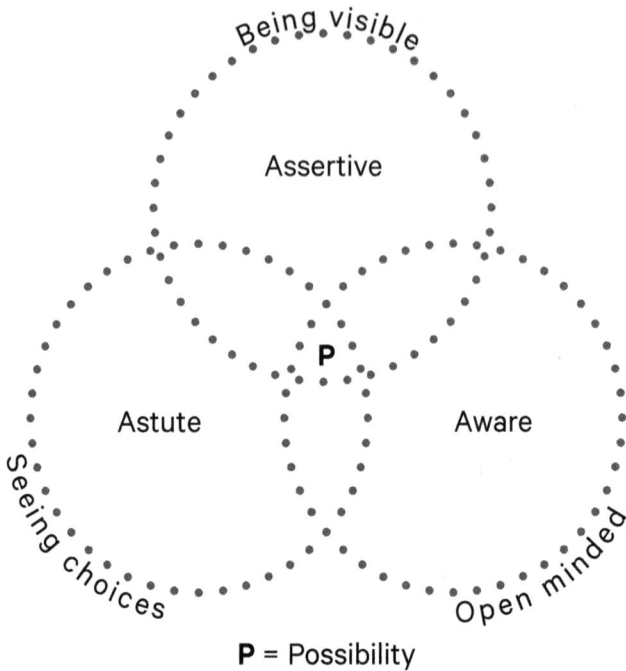

Being visible assists women to position themselves for new possibilities. This Assertive approach means being proactive in seeking out new networks, mentoring relationships, and working on self-development to learn new skills. My clients make real progress when they allow themselves the permission and the time to work on strategies that make them visible and noticed by others. There are many examples of this, including taking on new projects, presenting at conferences, attending new events and so on. When the two mindset factors of Awareness and Assertiveness combine, women are in **Scanning** mode, looking closely at opportunities with an open mind, and keeping themselves visible to those who can help them achieve their goals.

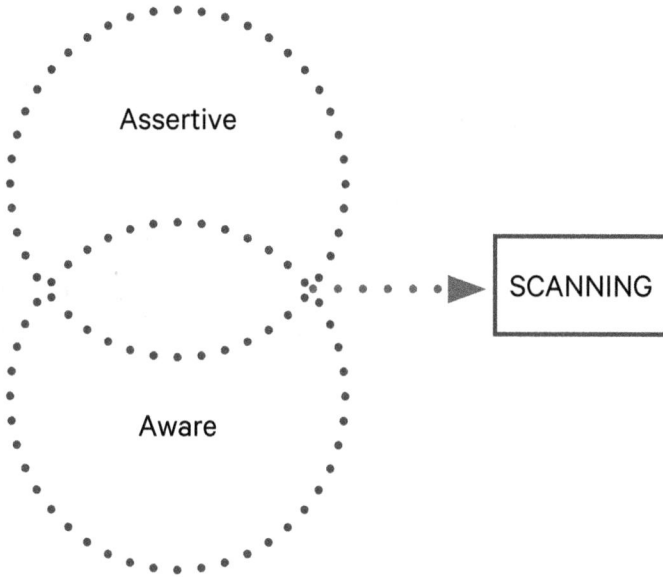

The definition of **Astute** in this model describes women who have developed a clear picture of the various choices they have. They no longer feel trapped in a role or a lifestyle. They understand their own values, how those values align with their work, or the options they might pursue to gain alignment in the future. When this mindset is combined with Awareness, women are in **Seeing** mode: they are aware of the choices available to them, and they are keeping an open mind about these.

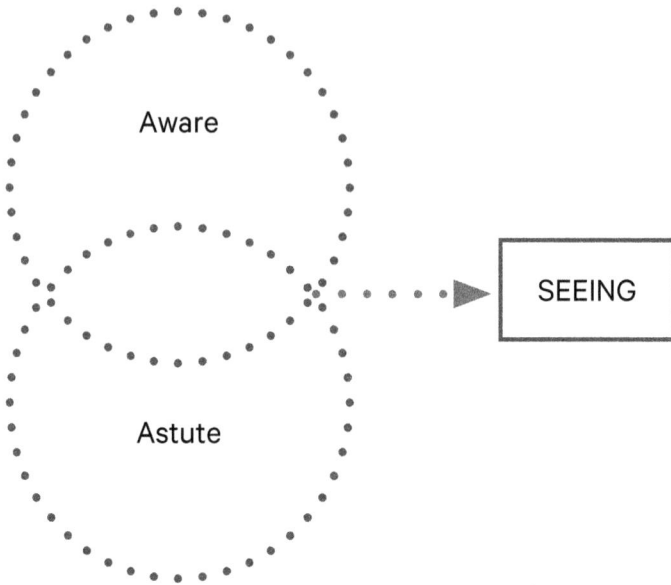

Aware

Astute

SEEING

When combined with Assertiveness, women can move towards
Sought mode, when they are clear about the available options best
for them and keeping in sight of those who can assist them with their
desired future. Then they are sought out for their skills and talents.

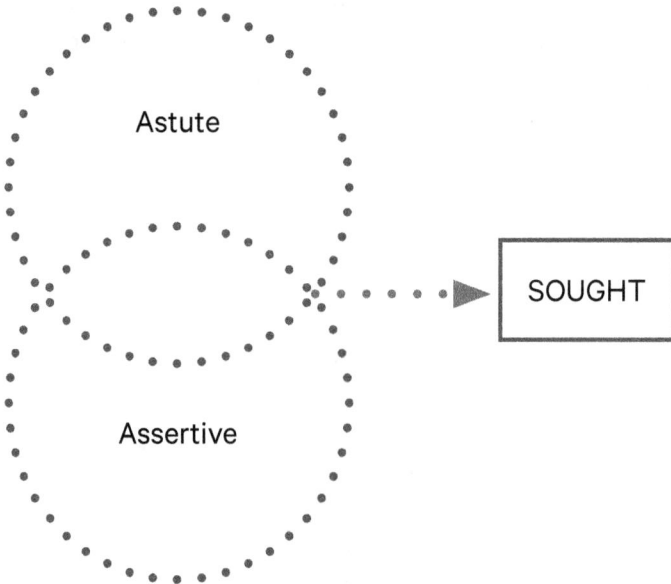

Astute

Assertive

SOUGHT

The significant difference I see in my practice, and with the women I speak to and interview, is that they make time to reflect on these issues. They consider their career development as real work, and give it time and priority.

They are not necessarily looking to climb a career ladder – they are seeking career fulfillment, and to maximise their potential.

So why am I writing about Possibility? What inspired me to think up a Possibility Model? It could be the warm, fuzzy feeling it gives me. It could be the legacy of writing this book. It might be the thought that the book might change just one life. Actually, it is all of those things, but more importantly, it's about the desire to see rural women activate their own possibilities.

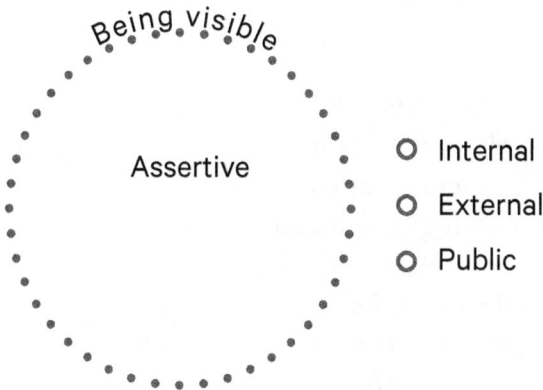

Being visible

Assertive

O Internal

O External

O Public

The first component I have outlined in the Possibility Model is being Assertive. I am defining it, in this instance, as making yourself visible for opportunities. For me, there are three types of visibility at play. The first relates to self-knowledge, and is internal. If you are visible to yourself, you know yourself well enough to make better and more informed choices in your career.

I have called the second type of visibility, external. This is being visible to outsiders or those people immediately around you.

Examples might include putting your hand up for higher duties placements, attending events, chairing organisational committees, or leading a new project. The more visible you can be within the organisation or group, the more people will recognise your skills and talents and can see you have an aspiration.

Women are generally fearful and uncomfortable about this type of visibility. Carole Sankar says we are more comfortable ending a relationship than we are asking for a pay rise. The desire to be seen as 'the good girl', not asking for too much, not stepping above where we should be, and not being egotistical or boastful, means we often avoid external visibility. Knowing ourselves well, and the issues that will push these buttons for us, is helpful in overcoming this challenge. Knowing our values and why we are being visible is also incredibly helpful, and enables us to be positioned in the right ways, strategically and deliberately.

Finally, its equally important to be visible publicly. This is a much wider arena where you are positioning for a much bigger audience. Examples might include attending and presenting papers at conferences, reviewing and creating a more relevant LinkedIn profile, posting on social media about relevant topics associated with your desired role, and so on. If you want to be head-hunted for your desired job, this is where you need to step up the public visibility. Jane Anderson, to whom I referred earlier, is one of the foremost thought leaders in this space in Australia. She writes about it in her book *Connect*[1], and teaches this in her online courses.

MEET GEORGIE

One of my coaching clients found that her success came from stepping her way through this process. Her early work with me focused on self-knowledge; values identification, strengths analysis and knowing her learning preferences. She built her internal visibility for herself, and took on some higher level work with her employer, making it clear that she was interested in more senior roles in the future. She has since acted in higher duties jobs and was offered the chance to join a professional network in her specialist area, which she now chairs. This public visibility has meant she is more widely known in the sector, recognised as having expertise and knowledge, and as someone with a big future in the industry. Her employers are keen to keep her engaged and to provide new opportunities because her reputation has grown externally. She was recently approached by another organisation about an upcoming role and following an application, she was successfully appointed. Her possibilities have tripled as a consequence.

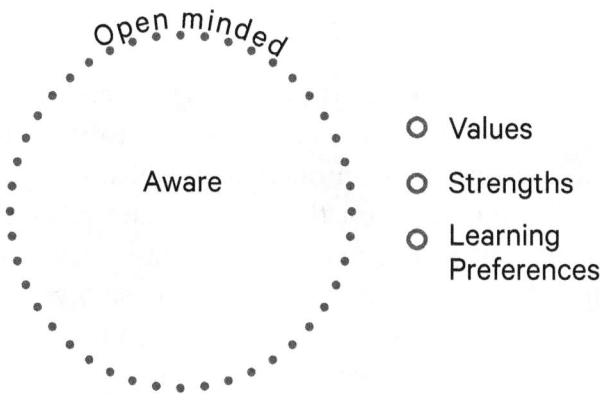

Open minded

Aware

O Values

O Strengths

O Learning
   Preferences

To my mind, there are three key elements in creating Awareness for Possibility. These are knowing your values, knowing your strengths, and knowing your learning preferences.

It's important to understand your values and what drives you. There are a myriad of values exercises you can undertake, some of them quite complex and others very simple. In my view, it doesn't matter which method you use. The critical step is to know what they are.

When you have identified your core values and written about what they mean for you, you can be more aware of the possibilities open to you. I have included a simple values discovery exercise at the end of this chapter. Many companies use these exercises with clients all the time, to help them discover their own possible options.

It's just as important to know your strengths. When you can play to your best strengths you can achieve more. We all have weaknesses or areas to develop. However, when we can maximise our strengths, our weaknesses all but disappear, or are well hidden. Knowing your strengths helps you position yourself more effectively and aim toward the right roles for you. Coupled with knowing your values, it means a stronger overall picture of how you can move towards your goals. There are also numerous strengths identification exercises you can do, and a simple one is included below, in the exercises section.

The third element is knowing your learning preferences. By this, I don't mean the traditional ideas of visual, auditory or kinesthetic etc. I mean knowing the environment in which you learn more effectively. This might be on the job, in quiet reflection when you download your experiences, or it might be via direction or instruction. When you know this about yourself, you can pitch toward the type of environment that works best for your learning. A learning styles exercise is also included below.

You can see where I'm going here. Self-knowledge mastery will be the most important way you can spend your time if you are seeking to cut through the grass ceiling. Possibilities come from knowing self, and aspiring toward the opportunities best suited to you.

Seeing choices

Astute

O Immediate (quick wins)

O Medium term

O Long term

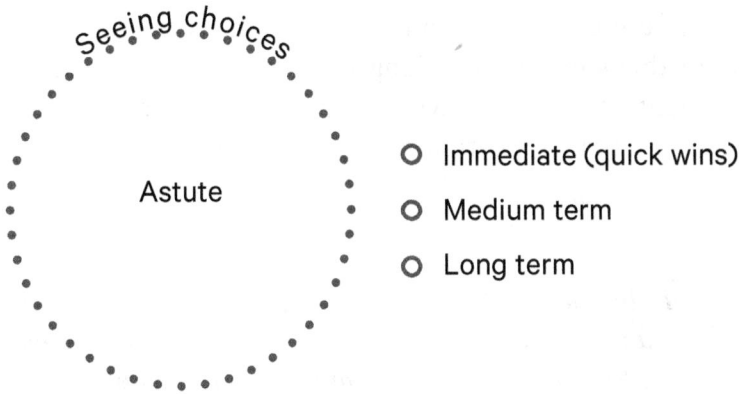

The third piece of the Possibility Model involves being Astute. It's here that we see choices becoming available to us. This builds on our self-knowledge and preparedness to be visible. Again, there are three elements involved, and these revolve around a time-frame.

Being astute in the immediate time-frame is about seeing quick wins. The choices available right now, and in the very near future. This could be the senior acting opportunity coming up, or project leadership. It might be joining a career-based group or network, or seeking a mentor.

The next time-frame is medium term. This is being astute and open to opportunities that may emerge in 6–12 months' time. Looking at roles that may become vacant, where someone might be taking an extended period of leave such as parental leave, or where a new role is being developed. Watching for these opportunities, building on your knowledge of self and being visible, means you can position more effectively for these occasions.

The third time frame is long term. This is where knowing values and strengths can be the most help. Knowing the roles you aspire to in your longer-term career, and the industries you might like to work within, means having an open-minded and practical approach to opportunities. There is time to do the building-block work, find some helpful connections, and join the right networks. It might involve further study, undertaking some coaching, or a leadership development program. Knowing what you need to do to be ready for the longer-term opportunities means being long-term astute.

MEET ALYSON

When I started coaching Alyson, she described herself as 'stuck in a rut'. She was working in a remote part of regional Australia. She had a great job that she valued highly. Alyson would be someone who could place herself at the 'Soaring' step of the ladder. However, after 10 years in the role, she felt there was no longer a stretch for her. Her intellectual stimulation was limited. She was making herself busy with administrative work, and feeling frustrated at other members of her team not pulling their weight. She had almost stopped delegating and was burying herself in tasks others could, and should, be doing.

Alyson told me that because she was so busy, she no longer attended networking functions in her capital city, or in the regional city a couple of hours from her work base. She felt lacklustre about everything. She didn't think she was performing at her peak. She felt she would never be able to apply for other senior jobs. Her mindset was that she was too out of date, not qualified enough, viewed as too 'rural' and 'just not ready'.

Through our detailed conversation, Alyson set the goals for her coaching program as exploring opportunities for growth and development in her job, determining a path forwards including 'where to' if she were to move on, and space to reflect on owning the role again.

Over several months of coaching, Alyson completed exercises, including a series of self-awareness interviews I set for her. These were undertaken with team members, external networks, and importantly, with her husband. Along with the reading and audio-visual materials I provided to Alyson, and the work we set between sessions, she discovered some useful information about herself, her mindset, and her patterns of behaviour.

By the mid-point of her coaching program, Alyson said she was proud of her ability to ask herself, 'do I need to do this?' in relation to tasks that other people in the team could take on. She was more focused on leading and renewing her networks. Not only was she more satisfied with her performance, she was happier, and bringing new business to the agency by reconnecting with people. She had some mojo back.

By the conclusion of her coaching program, Alyson was thriving again in her job. She had made some key decisions about her team. She was seeking appropriate support from her wider organisation. She was managing travel to networking events, which were useful to her role and for future prospects. She was doing the work she needed to do, and delegating effectively to team members.

Alyson described herself as less focussed on needing to move on. She was more interested in what else she could do with the job she had and enjoyed. She felt ready for new opportunities if they emerged for her, but she wasn't feeling 'trapped' any longer. Our conversations had changed. Alyson had energy and vigour seeping from her. She literally bounced into the room and lit it up when we were face-to-face.

Exercises:

- Try assessing your values with this simple exercise from the Barrett Centre https://survey.valuescentre.com/survey.html?id=s1TAEQUStmx-pUIle-ma6Q

- Log on to the University of Pennsylvania Authentic Happiness Questionnaire Center, register, and take the *VIA Survey of Character Strengths* to find out more about your top five strengths https://www.authentichappiness.sas.upenn.edu/user/login?destination=node/434

- Explore your learning style by taking the *VAK Learning Styles Self-Assessment Questionnaire* from Swinburne University http://www.swinburne.edu.au/stuserv/workshops/onlinematerials/Web%20Effective%20Study%20Skills_files/1VAK%20assessment.pdf

CHAPTER 11

MENTORS AND COACHES

You have shifted your mindset to growth, and your locus of control to internal. You've examined fear, risk, curiosity, and boldness. You've explored the Possibility Mindset. You've decided to use comparisons for positive goal-setting. Now, you're ready to work out your support strategies.

Mentoring has become one of the most popular forms of developing individuals. "It's almost universally held that mentoring is advantageous – indeed essential – for getting ahead. But that can be a dangerous perspective. Mentoring, if not managed thoughtfully and wisely, can derail your career." [1]

What happens when women can't find mentors to help them develop their careers? We know that women's aspirations and confidence erode at mid-career.[2] This is often the time when mentors and role models are least likely to be obvious. It's when we focus intently on our work, but not always our developmental needs.

Wendy Murphy[3] writes about finding role models when they are not immediately obvious. Murphy lists several factors to look for in seeking out role models:

- Observe the behaviours that are working for those people you admire.
- Focus on the behaviours you think you can emulate.
- Try things out.

- Get feedback.

- Look externally.

- Learn continuously.

I'd like to expand on these.

Murphy says we need multiple mentors—a 'personal board of directors'. I describe this as a Champions Map. This is an exercise I ask participants to do in my women's workshops. The map gives women the personal board of directors that Murphy writes about.

In workshops, I describe the importance of women being open to new opportunities. This means seeking out people who are best placed to be mentors, based on their behaviours. Identifying the personal traits that work for them can be instructive.

It is also important for women to remain visible to others. This includes testing behaviours and working styles; first in a trusted environment, and later in new situations, as confidence grows. This requires being open to feedback. With role models or mentors, women can check in about whether they need to tweak certain behaviours, and where they have learned most.

Women can be effective in seeking role models outside their work place if they are astute. Without mentors readily at hand in their own organisations, it's important to seek out people they can shadow at meetings and events, and connect with at networking functions.

Part of making career choices possible is finding champions to help you get there. Keep aspiring high. Seek the people who can help you build your confidence, and inspire your growth mindset. Complete your Champions Map (see below), and go for gold by doing a second one. Suddenly, your role models ARE obvious and you have a list of how you can best learn from them.

Exercise:

Complete your Champions map:

- Take an A4 piece of paper, and trace around one hand.
- At the top of each finger and the thumb, list a person you consider one of your champions.
- Try to find at least 3 people, and fist pump if you get to all 5.
- Now, along the length of each finger, write how that person can help you. This shows the ways that person is currently your champion.

Like mentoring, coaching has become the tool of choice in management development in recent years. It is established as a standard in some industries. There are significant benefits to individuals and organisations from coaching,[4] including:

- Revealing new talents or opportunities.
- Inspiring team members to coach others.
- Shifting culture in a positive forward direction.
- Supporting diversity initiatives.
- Assisting succession planning.
- Attracting and retaining talented people.
- Boosting morale.

The International Coach Federation cites research proving that people see significant benefits from coaching. This graphic from their web site provides a summary.

80%	73%	72%	67%
Improved self-confidence	Improved relationships	Improved communication skills	Improved life/ work balance

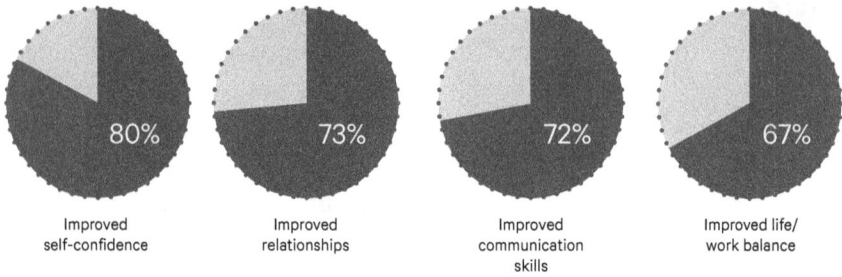

Beata Staszkow[5] describes several ways in which executive coaching improves people's performance. Staszkow says that coaching assists people see their talents, and provides a sounding board. She contends it helps executives develop and refine their 'soft' skills.

Engaging a coach is an important decision, and often a sizeable investment. Some of my clients tell me they have long thought about hiring a coach. They say they hesitated to commit because of the perceived risk of engaging the 'wrong' coach.

If you are seeking a coach for yourself, you can minimise this risk in several ways.

- Think about what you need from coaching. Make a list of your objectives. This equips you to talk with prospective coaches about how they propose to help you.

- Look for a coach who has studied to build their experience and refines their skills regularly. Ask them if they have their own coach/mentor, and if they undertake professional development and supervision.

- Read testimonials, for example, on the coach's website or on LinkedIn. Ask for references.

- Ensure you feel a sense of trust. It's important that coaching is a positive and energising experience.

PART 3

REGIONAL WOMEN CUTTING THROUGH

CHAPTER 12

CASE STUDIES

'Whether you come from a council estate or a
country estate, your success will be determined
by your own confidence and fortitude'.

—attributed to Michelle Obama

There are too many women for me to add to this book as case studies. There are women I know well, have met once or twice, or whom I've never met but have been told about. There are women I likely don't know about at all. All over regional Australia, readers will have examples of inspiring women who have cut through the grass ceiling. My intent in this section is to profile some very different women. They are diverse in age, culture, educational attainment, industry sector and interests. The common denominator is that they grew up in rural or regional Australia, and they have made their own possibility.

JESS JONES

I had the pleasure of interviewing Jess Jones, founder of Soar Collective, as she was driving to Ballarat to host an event for business women. Jess and I immediately found a strong connection, and her story below illustrates why she is such an important case study for this book.

Soar Collective's focus is on building an engaged and supportive community of businesswomen who, by sharing their successes and failures, can learn from, and empower each other. The Soar Collective manifesto includes a statement that the future of the regional economy is in women, and a commitment to supporting and connecting regional business women.

On 6 February 2017, Soar Collective initiated the inaugural Regional Businesswomen's Day. The #riseforregional campaign reached thousands of people, and raised the profile of regional and rural women in the Australian economy in an unprecedented way.

Jess Jones was born in outer Melbourne, and spent most of her childhood and adolescence in Gippsland. Her parents made a 'tree change' to Maffra in 1988, for her father to take up a new post playing football for the Maffra Eagles. Her mother opened a retail business. It was a big relocation for the family, and Jess suspects her mother felt it most, leaving behind her support networks for a rural environment. Jess reflects on the risks her parents took at that time, including starting a small business in a community unknown to them. Jess' mother was one of three women involved in the local chamber of commerce at the time, and in Jess' view, they didn't have much of a voice in decision-making. The business didn't go as well as planned, and the financial impact affected the family in various ways.

Jess was at secondary school in Sale, and aged 16, when her parents' marriage ended. She was expelled from school in Year 11, and her parents gave her the choice of continuing her education at another school or finding a job.

Jess says she never fitted an academic profile, and staying at school was not a good choice for her then. She had always loved sport, creative arts and music. She remembers her frustration on often asking her dad why she couldn't play footy, and why girls didn't have football teams. She was also perplexed about why there were no women in industries such as engineering—her father's chosen trade. Jess was so determined to play AFL football that she started the first girls' team at her school, which she co-captained. Her old school continues to offer the sport to this day, and the girls compete in the School Sports Victoria competition most years. (Jess shares my delight in the recent Women's AFL competition getting started across Australia, and the recognition women players are achieving.)

Jess chose to leave school; she went into a retail traineeship with a fast food chain. She struggled through the early months. Eventually though, she grew to love the job, realising she enjoyed the teamwork, processes, and results that a team could achieve when working well together.

At aged 17, Jess left home to live with her boyfriend. She kept working in retail, but at times missed her school friends and their social activities, including singing in local bands, with a view to reaching stardom in the big smoke. She became engaged, yet couldn't really settle into the life she was living. At 19, she split with her fiancé. Jess says she was 'fearful of being stuck in a rural life with small children', and maybe becoming trapped without having spread her wings.

Jess saw herself in the city chasing the bright lights. At that time, she was working in music retail having been the youngest person in Australia, in that chain, appointed to a store manager role. After a short stint exploring Queensland, she transferred to Melbourne with the chain, and continued working in retail and hospitality.

In her early 20s, Jess recalls sitting on a tram on her commute home, and having her 'epiphany'. She thought about how she could be doing more with her life, and making a better future. She began investing in personal and professional development, and saving some money. She no longer wanted to be living 'pay to pay'.

Jess had a dream of working in the United States for none other than Donald Trump, in his business empire. She found out that she couldn't secure an interview without a Green Card, and she couldn't get a Green Card without a job. So, in her late 20s, she travelled to New York City with an intention to spend a year exploring the world. Instead, she fell in love with New York and stayed. She worked in hospitality roles in the Upper West Side, managing venues for more than 50 hours per week. Jess thrived. She describes this year as 'when I finally grew into womanhood'.

Jess came home to Australia to reflect on her life plans. She worked for a time in events management and in corporate events. When Jess became pregnant with her first child, she started her own wedding and events styling and planning business. It was launched six weeks before she delivered her baby son. As Jess said, 'I never do things by halves.'

It was then time to make another change. Jess and her partner decided that to afford their own home, they would need to leave St Kilda and move farther out of Melbourne. They chose to spend a period with her partner's parents on the Mornington Peninsula, to save money. Jess was a little shocked by the lack of services and the isolation compared with the city, but she drew on her childhood experiences to make connections. She sought out other business owners in industries like hers, who were, incidentally, all women. She started meeting for coffee with this new network. Jess says she was surprised to find such a warm welcome and preparedness to sit down and talk together. She said when she had tried this approach in the city, it had been much harder to connect, and people weren't so forthcoming with information or support.

Jess found the networking groups she went to didn't resonate with her, and she couldn't afford to continue driving to Melbourne to be part of the groups and events with which she used to be involved. Through a local businesswomen's Facebook group, she initiated a conversation about *meeting up* and it eventuated, with 12 local women attending a morning tea event, who were keen to get together and talk about new ways of supporting each other in business. This was her chance to share what she had learned, and provide value to other people. On 8 May 2014, the Soar Collective, as an infant organisation, held its first event. Three years on, Jess loves her work and the women she meets all over regional Victoria.

Jess believes that her childhood in the country helped make Soar Collective possible. She remembers being a natural leader organising the neighbours' children and her cousins (all younger than her) to undertake activities. She feels the safety of that environment, and the freedom she had, influenced her view of opportunities and encouraged her to take risks. While she feels there are some disadvantages to country life, such as the complete lack of anonymity as a teenager (!) there is a positive flipside.

Jess now lives on the Peninsula with her partner and their young son and baby daughter. I asked Jess for three things she would say to a 16-year-old girl living in Maffra today. She said:

1. Don't be limited by your surroundings – both physically and metaphorically. Don't allow others (even those who love you) to place limits on you through their influence. This includes your parents, best friends, teachers, and others you look up to. Remember, their experiences and expectations are theirs, not yours.

2. Wherever you can, take opportunities for personal development. Read books, and keep learning, always. Be well-informed. School education isn't everything. It doesn't

matter if you don't want to go to university. Life will simply be better for you if you allow yourself to learn and develop.

3. Find your mentors. Find them at an early age. Mentors aren't just for adulthood. They're not just for early careers. You need them (and different ones) throughout life. Don't be afraid to ask people to be your mentor.

Jess' favourite quote is by Lisa Messenger: 'Have unwavering self-belief and the rest will follow'. Jess says that "although this might be a cliché, it is always the first step. Trust your own judgement, otherwise that lack of confidence in yourself will be on show to others. Be your own team and find champions who absolutely believe in you. These won't always be your family or friends".

Jess is an avid note-taker. She says this has helped her reflect through her life on her history of ideas and plans. She told me about a 'goose-bump moment' where she recently opened her journal to see all her plans for supporting others through a network of sorts, from as early as 10 years ago. She realised she is living her dream, and Soar Collective is the product of many years' thinking and passion. I'm grateful the planet has Jess Jones on it.

CATHY MCGOWAN

Cathy McGowan AO MP, was born in Albury and raised on her family's dairy farm near Wodonga. She went to school in the district and, later, in Melbourne. She started her career as a teacher before becoming an electoral assistant to a member of parliament. Cathy was then employed in the Department of Agriculture. She has been an academic, and has run her own consulting business.

Cathy purchased her farm in North East Victoria and continued her business and volunteer commitments. She was a regional councilor for the Victorian Farmers' Federation, a President of Australian Women in Agriculture, and a director of a credit union. Since

2013, Cathy has been the Member for Indi, a seat in the Australian House of Representatives. She retained the seat in the 2016 Federal Election.

In 1996–97, Cathy undertook the Australian Rural Leadership Program. When I interviewed her in August 2016, Cathy described this time as a 'turning point'. She said she learned the importance of listening to hear—to trust that she could listen and accept different viewpoints. This value became an important factor in Cathy's campaign for Indi. The campaign team developed an agreed set of values, one of which was respect. It was important to Cathy that her team would never 'bad-mouth the opposition'. She wanted people to have the confidence to engage in constructive conversations about issues with constituents.

She feels the community 'harnessed its own local energy', as is often the case in communities when an issue is important to people. In Cathy's view, the campaign increased young peoples' interest in politics, and their direct involvement in democracy.

Cathy says it's important to avoid the trap of comparing rural and regional life with life in the city. 'My life never did have anything to do with the city,' she said. She rejects the view that there is something different about people in regional areas, and the assumption that there are fewer choices to make.

Cathy says she had lots of examples in her younger life of people living successfully in a rural environment. There was nothing unusual or unexpected about going off to study, and returning to take up employment. At the time, there was 'nothing hard about that', and it was expected people would do so.

For Cathy, it is possible to live a successful life in a regional area because of the other people living around her, going about their daily lives, in business and in the community. It's where she wants to be, with her family and her friends.

She described it as a case of managing the circumstances to enable the life she wants. 'How could I live in the country and keep my lifestyle here, make enough money for the things I wanted to do?' Cathy's message to young women is 'look around you – there are many examples of great people doing great things', and it is entirely possible to be successful.

JENNY HAMMETT

Jenny Hammett is one of the most professional women I know. There is a calmness and self-contained confidence about Jenny. At the same time, she shows a steely resilience that, in my view, has served her well throughout the various roles she has played in regional Australia.

Jenny is the former Victorian State Director of the National Party. Jenny grew up in Traralgon, where she attended public primary and secondary schools.

Jenny has had a diverse career, including time at Target as a Human Resources Manager, an electorate officer for a Federal MP, an Adviser to a Minister for Science, the CEO of a not-for-profit educational service, and a Communications Director in the utilities sector.

Having developed a strong interest in politics, Jenny stood as a candidate for the National Party in the Legislative Assembly seat of Morwell, at the 2002 Victorian State election. She stood again, unsuccessfully, at the November 2006 election in the Legislative Council region of Eastern Victoria.

In 2010, Jenny became the State Director of the National Party, a position she held until her resignation in 2014.

I first met Jenny properly in 2002, when she worked for the then Member for Gippsland, and I was leading a regional development agency. We commenced a long and fruitful working relationship—one that I am grateful for in a multitude of ways. Jenny has been a wonderful ally and friend, and I seek her wise counsel often.

I asked Jenny to be a case study for this book in mid-2016. This is her reflection of cutting through the grass ceiling.

It was the late 80's and Jenny had the 'perfect' job for a mum with young children, and no qualifications. She was a kindergarten assistant working pretty much school hours, and loved the job. It worked for that time. She knew, though, that it wouldn't satisfy her curiosity about the world forever.

Something was driving her to look to the future, to think beyond the kindergarten and take a step forward to forge a new opportunity for herself. Education was the key. At 28, she enrolled as a mature-aged student to study part-time for a Bachelor of Arts. The third of four girls, she was the first person in her family to enroll in tertiary education. It didn't go down too well with some of the family, especially her mother, who thought that she should be concentrating on her young family. While Jenny's family was very important to her, she wanted and needed to take a path that varied from the one her mother had taken.

That was the first time Jenny realised she wanted to pursue something different. There has been a second, a third and a fourth time. Jenny left the kindergarten in 1993 and took a three-month contract as a publicity officer for a disability organisation. When the contract ran out, she had no idea what would be next. A store-based human resource manager in a national retail chain challenged and taught her more than she could have imagined, and empowered her to pursue other career opportunities.

Jenny says, 'the gift it gave me was the practical knowledge and the management experience to overcome the regional inferiority complex I had previously carried whenever I ventured to Melbourne for a head office meeting.'

Jenny describes an innate need to experience personal growth, and the unfailing support of her husband who, when she was consumed by anxiety over her decision and what it would mean, said 'just do it'.

Jenny recalls the support and encouragement of a number of women outside her immediate family was also a key factor in helping her to overcome self-doubt and fear. One of those women was a teacher from her children's school. On hearing of Jenny's enrolment at university, she spoke encouragingly, and 'her words came back to me time and time again throughout the years that I was studying, working and raising a family, as a gentle yet strong reminder that I could do this.'

Jenny also had a number of male mentors, although not formal, who provided continuous encouragement and imparted a blend of commonsense and profound wisdom. 'The belief of others in me was stronger than my belief in myself. It was their belief in me, and my commitment to not letting them down, that enabled me to achieve and succeed.'

Jenny's initial decision was born amidst a clash of values, the family values that had dominated her young adulthood and early married life, and the emerging values of a new era for women in Australia. She describes herself as caught between what had been, and what might be. She chose the latter, though 'not without enduring considerable anxiety, a fair smattering of criticism, and a good dose of self-doubt.'

Jenny believes values have been a defining factor in the path of her career. The consequential stress and angst of a values clash within an executive management team is something she has experienced on a number of occasions. It has been the impetus for her to take a new direction more than once.

In the early 90s, Jenny recalls reading Stephen Covey's *Seven Habits of Highly Effective People*. She believes that changed the way she interpreted the world around her and how she participated in it. It made a significant difference to her, and caused her to examine the relevance and importance of values in our personal and working lives. She was still working at the kindergarten when she read it, and 'reflecting on it now, it may well have been the cause of my determination to do something different, and do it differently.'

Jenny told me that having an open mind is " ... crucial, being open to the opportunities that present themselves and embracing them even when you don't feel ready for it, allows you to stretch well beyond the limits you think you are capable of. There are times when you stretch just that bit too far and you feel the slap-back, or you bounce about trying to find direction. What you are really doing, though, is training in resilience—the bounce back. Being open to the learning, reflecting on the experience, finding the better way, comes to an open mind, not a closed one."

"It was absolutely a key factor for me. I started out with a need for personal growth, and left the kindergarten thinking I might become a teacher. I went into retail because someone I know told me I should apply for the job, that my skills were suited to it. I didn't recognise my ease in working with others as a skill; it took someone else's encouragement to get me there."

Jenny enrolled to do a Diploma of Education while she was in retail, and had planned an exit strategy from the store with the full support of the company's senior management. She had moved on to training, as a prelude to teaching, when the unexpected arose - an opportunity to apply for a role working for a local member of parliament. Again, it was someone else that suggested she could do the job. She saw it as an opportunity to work for Gippsland, and to work within our system of democracy, two things she is deeply passionate about. She deferred her Diploma enrolment and never took it up again.

Working with this parliamentarian was a unique experience, a great gift of learning for Jenny on so many levels, it revealed pathways she had never imagined. 'If I had not been open to embracing that opportunity when it arose, then the incredible journey my career has taken me on would just not have occurred.'

When (practically) speaking about the other support, Jenny describes needing support at home. She was working in Canberra for a good part of the time, and when she was in Gippsland she was travelling at least an hour and a half every day. She and her husband had a new home, and she wanted to maintain it and establish a garden. Jenny says, "I had never envisaged someone else cleaning my home, it didn't fit with my image of a good wife and mother. What I discovered was a need to re-evaluate an image that didn't fit with the new circumstance of our life. Managing the guilt was not nearly as difficult as I had contemplated it would be. Having a cleaner was empowering for our family; it gave us back something so precious—time. And it was empowering for our employee; it enabled her to work within the framework of her family's priorities. She was a treasured find and a great support and resource for us all."

Beyond that, Jenny notes advances in technology as important. "It's importance was emerging in 1999, and over the course of the next five years the advances for working from home were significant."

Finally, Jenny notes: "For me, it is very important to acknowledge that from the beginning I had the security of another income in our home. That was freedom, it provided a safety net—if I failed, we wouldn't starve. I didn't fail; I thrived, we all did. I was spared the anxiety of being the sole income provider and was able to stretch as far as I could with that security supporting me."

LEAH METHER

Leah Mether is a 'fuel generation plant'. The energy emanating from this woman is enough to power a small town. In fact, in some ways, it does (more on that below).

I first met Leah in early 2016. Her sister had met me and suggested that some of my work was like that of Leah's, and she suggested we meet. I reached out on LinkedIn, and we made a breakfast date. That was a fateful decision. Leah and I have subsequently gone on to collaborate on several projects. She is a great supporter and mentor for me, and I'd like to think I provide the same for her.

Leah is the owner of Methmac Communications. Her career includes periods as a newspaper journalist and corporate communications manager, before she struck out on her own as a communications consultant following the birth of her first child in 2010. Since then, Leah has worked extensively in several regional industries, including the energy, water, health, and education sectors. She has drawn extensively on her strong local network to build her business—from a few occasional jobs with the aim of keeping her skills current while she focussed on being a mum, to a thriving business with a diverse range of clients, including large corporates, small businesses, education services, community groups and individuals. She also runs communications workshops, media training, motivational seminars, and is an experienced MC and public speaker.

Leah describes herself as ' ... the mother of three young boys, a wife, community volunteer, business owner, fiction writer, fitness lover, and chocoholic'. Her major passion is helping other people "get the most out of life by removing the roadblocks to success, overcoming self-doubt, controlling how they respond to life's challenges, and achieving their dreams with effective goal setting." Phew!

Before this life, Leah took some gap time. On leaving university, Leah packed her bags and drove herself off into the sunset to travel around Australia, alone. She did this for 12 months, working in various towns in a range of jobs from bar-tending in a remote roadhouse in central Australia, to door-to-door sales in Darwin, and working as supervisor at a large restaurant in Perth. It was a life-changing experience that fostered in Leah an 'eyes wide open' perspective on the world around her. It helped to concrete her aspiration to be her best self.

What strikes me most about Leah is her commitment to excellence. In working alongside her, and talking with her extensively, I see a woman on a mission to expel mediocrity from regional communications. Leah shows an in-built desire to kill off any view that women can't have the best of all worlds in regional areas. She is a living, breathing, walking version of the woman who has created her own destiny.

Yet, anyone who thinks that she has it easy would be wrong. This life that Leah has built is not shiny and glossy all the time. She has had her fair share of hurdles to jump, tragedies to cope with, and personal illness to live with. She is an ardent supporter and volunteer speaker for *beyondblue*, as her husband battled depression following a severe back injury due to a motor vehicle accident.

Despite, and perhaps because of this, Leah gets up every day to live the best life she can. She stays fit by training hard, she is committed to her relationship with her husband, sons, and extended family, and she helps her local community in many ways.

In 2015, Leah and her cousin-in-law Kate launched a public campaign regarding rural kindergarten funding in the State of Victoria. Victorian kindergarten services are two-thirds funded by the State Government, and the remaining third funded through parent fees and fundraising. The Federal Government also contributes a small amount of funds. This used to leave rural kindergartens with a funding shortage to cover basic operational costs, depending on enrolment numbers. Through their campaign, they achieved a change in government policy, which now means the State Government is investing $4.4 million over four years (2016–2020) in rural communities.[1]

Thinking of the Possibility Model, I see Leah's attributes everywhere. She is always willing to put herself forward, and is not afraid to be visible. Leah stays in touch with her connections, develops her network, and places high value on the people she knows. This means when it's time to call on them for a favour or for help, they are very willing to be involved. She has worked hard on her communication skills, and her emotional intelligence. Leah knows who she is, and her strengths and areas for improvement. This helps her to be astute, and to have a clear view of the best way for her to act on her aspirations.

Leah is a wonderful example of a regional woman who has cut through the grass ceiling. From her earliest days at work, she has had her eyes on something bigger. She has aspired to grow, learn, and take new risks in her career and her life. She is a true example for regional girls of being Possible.

I'm deeply proud to call her my friend.

MELISSA HAMMOND

Mel Hammond has been my hairdresser for a long time. While she has done my hair many times, she has been the owner of the salon I attend, for more than a decade. In writing Mel's story, it could be said that she has cut through, quite literally!

When I first met Mel, she was a young woman who had returned from a period overseas and had come home to Gippsland. Mel had been working in Manchester, in the United Kingdom, while her partner had played professional cricket there. On their return, Mel found a job in a local salon that had a steady clientele and was owned by an absentee businesswoman interstate.

Essentially, to secure her own job and those of some staff she worked with, Mel embarked on a very brave venture. She took over the business, and relocated it with a new name. Ten years on, another larger premises, a sizeable staff, a marriage to her partner, and the birth of two little boys, Mel owns one of the most successful salons in the area.

I interviewed Mel and asked her what it was that made her think her big leap into salon ownership was possible.

Mel grew up in the township of Moe. She attended Lowanna College, and in Year 11, her family relocated to Traralgon. Mel decided to commute back to Lowanna each day to finish her school year.

While Mel originally wanted to be a flight attendant, she was told being so petite, she wouldn't be accepted by any airline as she didn't meet the height requirements. So, Mel chose to do hairdressing during school work experience, and she loved the salon environment.

While still at school, Mel's early employment experiences were in the fast food industry. She absolutely believes she learned her customer service skills in these outlets. She says they were a wonderful training ground for her. (Now, as an employer, she notices people who have had that early experience have better customer service orientation, and she looks for this in their skill base.)

On leaving school, Mel was employed full time in a large retail appliances and furnishings chain. She became the small appliance manager at aged 18. Clearly, her training in customer service and sales had paid off. Mel recalls selling a coffee machine to a woman opening a hair salon. Through the conversation that day, the woman invited Mel to apply for an apprenticeship. She did, and got the job. She continued working weekends in her other job.

When Mel had almost finished her apprenticeship, she met her partner, Kent. He was on his own journey and was due to start playing county cricket in Manchester. Mel moved overseas with Kent, where she worked in hairdressing and hospitality for the 6 months they were away. Mel loved the experience of meeting new people, working for a large hotel chain, and seeing another part of the world in a big multicultural city.

Mel and Kent returned to Australia and settled in Traralgon. She went to the local TAFE college to finish her hairdressing training modules so she could qualify for work in Australia. Mel worked from home for a time, and then got a job at the salon where I first met her, in 2005.

Mel found her place, quickly developing close connections with several team members, including one woman she employs to this day, as her salon manager. When Mel realised that the salon was not likely to continue longer-term, she decided she would 'go for it' and set up on her own. She looked at shops, signed a lease, and contacted the interstate salon owner to suggest taking some staff with her. Others had already found new jobs. At that point, the owner decided to close the business, and Mel opened her new salon.

I asked Mel what it was that gave her the drive to make this significant move at an early age. She said 'nothing was ever enough. I always wanted more'. Mel says her early experiences of working part-time after school and throughout her apprenticeship gave her an opportunity to contribute to her family's income, and to have some funds for herself. She also recognised in herself a tendency to be easily bored when she had mastered something, thus looking for new challenges.

Mel says she didn't give herself time to be scared, and she didn't overthink her decision. She wanted to open the salon to see if it would work. In hindsight, she says, had she been older, it might have been more daunting, but she was "too excited at the time to see it ... I think I'm still like that, actually."

At that time, Mel sought the advice of small business support workers in State and Australian Government agencies, so she could absorb all the information she needed to know as a new business owner. To me as her client, even then, she seemed very clear on strategy and who she needed to engage to gather useful information.

Mel says it hasn't always been easy to run the business. She has had to move people on when things haven't worked out. Recruitment has, at times, been challenging. There are sometimes difficult customers. Good staff make choices to leave, too. She reflects, however, that in moments of stress, she has told herself "what you're panicking about right now won't matter in a week or two. There are other good people out there, and you can replace the person who's gone."

She tried opening another salon in a nearby town, but shut it down within a year. The manager of that site resigned a few weeks before Mel was to give birth to her second baby. She quickly realised she couldn't be in three places at once and available to everyone who required her attention. She had also found that two salons didn't mean twice the income. It was, at times, harder and costlier. Rather than seeing it as a 'fail', Mel says she is very glad to have tried a second salon, and about her clear decision to close it. It seems it was a great learning experience in many ways. Mel giggled, "It still makes me laugh when people tell me I'm loaded because I have my own business. That takes a long time, and it's not the main reason I'm here."

Mel says the best parts of her business journey have been watching younger people grow into their jobs. She loves bringing apprentices on board and seeing them through to graduation.

When I asked her what's next in her career, Mel noted her need to keep growing herself and her skills. Now, as the mum of 2 little boys, and with 10 years in the business, Mel has consolidated. She has her salon manager, and a business coach. She intends to focus on being the salon owner and parent for a few years, before she decides what else to try. This will also give space for others in the team to grow their skills. "They don't need me around all the time – they will be freer." She is open-minded about opportunities and where they might lead.

One of the things Mel is most proud of is that it's good for her sons to see their mother in her own business. She wants to encourage the boys to try new things, and to have perseverance to keep learning. This role modelling is important to Mel and Kent.

I asked Mel what advice she would give to young girls in preparing for their future. Here are her tips.

- Enjoy your time as a young person while it's here. Don't grow up too fast. Adult life will be waiting for you.

- Go for your dreams, and don't let anyone else tell you they're not possible.

- Learn to be self-supporting, and be prepared for some sacrifice. Save money. Have fun, for sure, but give up some fun to enable you to do the things you need to. I had to sell my car to get a business loan deposit. It was my dream car and I'd saved ages for it. The deposit was more important, so the car went. I bought a cheaper car to get me through. I sold another car later to buy my house block so I could build a home.

Mel Hammond is an example of almost every element in this book. I'm so glad to have met her all those years ago, and to have observed her growth as a business owner and a woman. Her infectious smile and welcoming hugs make me feel special every time I see her in the salon. She's a Gippsland Girl made Good—actually, Great.

LYNDA BERTOLI

I have known Lynda Bertoli professionally for almost twenty years. I first met Lynda through a regional development activity in which we were both engaged. I liked her instantly. Warm and engaging, with a great sense of humour, Lynda always seemed to me to be the epitome of a successful regional woman who could stand alongside the best in the nation, and beyond.

I'm not sure that she would see it this way. Lynda, in my view, tends to hide her light behind the proverbial bushel. She isn't all that keen on the limelight, and I'm even more appreciative of her agreeing to be in this book.

Lynda grew up in Newborough in an average family, with mum, dad, and a sister. She was educated locally and went on to have a career in the State Electricity Commission of Victoria (SECV) at Yallourn, in administration. This is where she met her husband, Ross, and they started their life journeys together.

Quite a lot has changed since then. Lynda still lives in Moe South, yet her horizons are much broader than those early days.

Until she retired from the firm in July 2017, Lynda was the managing director of the software company Sage Technology, with clients across Australia and internationally. These companies include Woodside, BAE Systems, Fortescue, Energy Australia, and

Rio Tinto. Most of Sage Technology's competition in the market is overseas-based. Lynda led a company of innovation and influence from her corporate base in Morwell.

Lynda and her then business partner started Sage technology in 1990, on leaving roles at the then State Electricity Commission of Victoria. When I interviewed Lynda, she recalled 'toddling around in a bright pink maternity smock and heels, moving computers and crawling around furniture so we could get the office set up.' Lynda was five months pregnant and had an 18-month-old son when the original computer consulting company commenced operations.

Over several years, Sage Technology grew into a business that provided IT infrastructure and software, and employed up to 50 staff. In more recent years, Lynda, and her co-director Peter Kingwill, decided to sell off the infrastructure arm of the company and move solely to software development. Their major work now is in developing and providing electronic permit to work software systems.

One of Lynda's clear passions is spreading the word about working from a regional Australian base. Being in IT, she feels that Sage Technology was one of the early companies that could flourish and develop without needing to be in a larger city. While new advances in technology mean that we can often now work anywhere, that wasn't always the case. Lynda and her team were groundbreakers in this regard, especially in regional Victoria.

Lynda is also deeply concerned about opportunities for young people in regional areas. That's why she tries to source as many of her staff as she can in the local area, helping to develop young people fresh out of university, or in graduate programs.

Having a future career in the region is important to many young people, and Lynda wants Sage Technology to continue its long tradition of making this possible.

Lynda believes in giving back to the community in which she has grown up and prospered. To this end, Lynda has been a long-time member of the Gippsland Emergency Relief Fund board, and is a Deputy President. She is a former board member of the Committee for Gippsland, the Monash University Gippsland Advisory Council, and the former Scope adult education board.

It has been important for Lynda to recognise her strengths and capacities along the way. Being a wife, mum, business owner/ company director, and a community volunteer means a juggling act. She believes in the power of knowing what we can commit to, and saying no. Lynda is clear that success comes from self-knowledge and committing to the few things she can do well, not overloading herself.

Having role models like Lynda Bertoli is so important for girls and young women in regional Australia. Having the opportunity to know her, and work alongside her, has been my privilege.

ANGELA BETHERAS

I met Angela Betheras at her Darnum home in mid-2016. I was surprised I'd never met Angela before, and slightly ashamed that I'd never visited her beautiful retail store, Nickelby, at Darnum on my regional travels.

Angela is full of life. The day we met, everything about her screamed *flat out, community-oriented, focused and driven.* She had just returned from a community meeting in a nearby township where she had been helping other business owners with ideas. When she caught her breath and sat down for coffee with me, she was warm and reflective about her grass ceiling journey.

Born in Labertouche, Angela grew up on her parents' beef property. She was educated in the region, and then in Berwick from Grade 5. After her secondary education, Angela went to start her career in the big smoke. She commenced at Country Road and the Just Group, prior to taking on a job, which was the pinnacle of her career, as the manager of the International Supply Chain for Australia's largest importer—bringing in the equivalent of a ship a week and working with all 29 companies in the group. In her late 30s, she decided it was time to do something different.

The pull to come 'home' was strong. Angela started off with a bed-and-breakfast venture in West Gippsland, which she managed while still working in the city full time. There came a point though, where she wanted to get right back to the land and run her own property.

Angela says she decided to start her alpaca farm due to her interest in farming fleece animals. She says she 'fell in love with and purchased my first alpacas in 2004.' Nickelby at Darnum now includes the farm, a retail shop, photographic studio, olive grove and café. She also has her own design range, *Nickelby Designs*.

The tree-change and farm life has not always been easy. The 2009 Black Saturday fires impacted West Gippsland. Angela is a Black Saturday survivor. This means she often considers the impact of natural disasters on other regions. and the people affected. For example, a year after Black Saturday, she hosted events at Nickelby, donating a percentage of sales from the day to raise funds for the women who were impacted by flooding in Charleton, Victoria in 2010.

In 2011, Angela won the RIRDC Victorian Rural Woman of the Year Award. With the bursary she received from this award, Angela worked with other women textile artists, who were also breeding alpacas, to form a network aimed at producing garments for export to China and the South-East Asian markets. Angela used the bursary to investigate opportunities for herself and other textile artists to export to China, and do a feasibility study into the merits of doing so.

A director of Lardner Park Events since 2011, Angela is currently the Chair of the Board. In her term on the Board, Angela has been the mastermind of the Women in Agriculture program, which is now held on the first day of Farm World each year. More than 200 women attend the lunch event each year, to network and listen to great rural woman and their stories. Angela considers working in a rural area to be a bonus. Being away from Melbourne has not been a barrier to her success. 'West Gippsland is an hour from the beach, an hour from the snow ... you can be in Collins Street at 9.00 am for a business meeting, and back home on the farm by 2.00 pm.'

Angela was frank with me. She said, in her view, there hadn't been many obstacles to her career. She felt she had been able to make the choices she wanted to pursue.

Her reflections on the grass ceiling were interesting. Having been in the fashion and retail industries for a considerable time, Angela's experiences are somewhat different to the other women in this book. She had certainly felt the impacts of burn-out, and working huge hours in a frenzied environment. She had met her fair share of challenging personalities, both men and women. She was direct. "You just can't listen to them. You have to do your own thing."

Angela's general view is that it's important to give things a go. Her personal values were a critical factor in helping her make the decision to create a new life for herself. She no longer wanted to be in the work cycle she was experiencing. She knew she had other options. Being on her own on a farm was slightly daunting. There are major tasks to be undertaken, and these require physical and mental strength and stamina.

Angela is grateful for the support of good neighbours and friends who assist her when needed. It seems to me that Angela appreciates kindness, and it goes a long way with her. I reckon it's karma. All the support and care she has offered to others (and still does) is delivered back to her by the universe.

Designing our own destiny isn't always going to be joyful or light-hearted. The message I take away from my wonderful encounter with Angela Betheras is that we should always listen to ourselves and believe that we can do it. Even on the days when it seems too hard, we need to hold on to the thought that drove us to get started with a new project or life change in the first instance.

Every day, Angela might be required to do something new, that she isn't sure of, and can't do YET. She keeps trying though, and masters the things important to her – whether they be running the property, her business, being a board director, or community change agent.

Angela Betheras is a great example of a woman with a growth mindset.

ROBBIE SEFTON

Robbie Sefton is a woman who values curiosity, authenticity, positivity, entrepreneurialism and perseverance. Robbie is the managing director of Seftons—a communications and corporate affairs agency she founded in 1990. From the time she began working, Robbie set out to prove it was possible to run a fulfilling and successful national business with highly-skilled team members from rural Australia.

In her biography, Robbie makes it clear that her vision for rural, regional and remote Australia is of a vibrant and flourishing place where people work in rewarding careers. Robbie doesn't just simply want this for herself. She is resolved to provide jobs and career opportunities for young people, particularly young women, in rural communities. Robbie is quoted as saying "I'm not doing this for my kids, (because I don't have any), I'm doing it for everyone's kids in the bush."

In 2013, Seftons won the Government Relations Consultancy of the Year (6+ staff) in the inaugural national Government Relations Awards. Through Seftons, Robbie has been involved in projects such as the Blueprint for Australian Agriculture 2013–2020, and the National Biodiversity Strategy. She is a graduate of the Australian Rural Leadership Program, and was awarded the 2002 RIRDC NSW Rural Woman of the Year.

A producer of wool, meat and grains with her partner, Alistair Yencken, on their farm near Tamworth, Robbie is also a member of numerous boards and advisory groups for governments, businesses and not-for-profits. Some examples include advisory boards for the Australian Taxation Office, the Reserve Bank of Australia, Woolworths, and the University of Southern Queensland.

She has also been involved as a board member with the National Australia Day Council (NADC) at a state and national level since 2006. Robbie is currently the Deputy Chair of the NADC. In 2017, Robbie noted her delight that "11 of the 32 finalists for this year's national awards hailed from rural and regional Australia".[2]

Robbie lists her five strategies for success as being:

1. Be driven by your vision.

2. Be courageous, resilient and tenacious.

3. Acknowledge with care and respect.

4. Be authentic: Walk the talk.

5. Be passionate, but with purpose.

KATE METHER

Kate Mether works in a business support role in a specialist school. She is the mum of three children, and has a busy family and work life.

In her early 20s, Kate started a herd improvement business in Gippsland called Nexus Herd Improvement, with funding from Holland. She started the business from scratch, and was the director. She was also responsible for hiring and firing.

Being in such a male-dominated industry was challenging enough, but to be the boss was a whole other matter.

Kate was generous in sharing her story for this book.

In the business, most of Kate's work days involved twice as many people questioning why she wanted to work in the herd improvement industry at all, than the number of people who were genuinely excited to see someone having a go at doing something they loved. Many of the people Kate worked with were so caught up in stereotypes of what a woman in her early 20s should want to do, that:

> They couldn't see I was actually happy and enjoying my job. My workmates and customers would apologise (continuously) for swearing at staff, heavy tanks, mud, cow manure, the weather, and overzealous dogs—all things that were part of a job I loved. Even after explaining that these were all part of my job, they never seemed to believe it. They thought they knew me better than I knew myself, because they thought they knew how all women thought and what all women preferred.

Of course, this lead to Kate being surrounded by people that made her question if she was in the wrong industry. Were mud and cow dung way more revolting than she thought? Were her customers only buying products and advice because she was female, and they thought they had a chance at hooking up? Was she a crazy farm kid that had grown up to be a crazy farm adult? Was she too weak to lug around 40kg tanks?

> After 18 months of listening and smiling and reassuring my customers and work mates that I was ok with all the things my job involved, I started to fear I was bullshitting myself. Surely, this many people couldn't be wrong. I was either a freak or delusional.

Kate says the more time she gave these thoughts, the more believable they seemed, and by the time she had decided to start Nexus, with the help of some overseas funding, she was convinced she was a fraud. Self-doubt had hit new levels, and she had convinced herself she was out of her depth. Kate said, 'Not once did I mention these thoughts to anyone, not even my partner. I was terrified I had wasted my time trying to carve a career in this industry.'

Kate recalls one afternoon driving home with a lot of negative questions whizzing around in her head. 'What if I fail, and I prove them all right?' She thought about this single question the entire drive. She decided she would need to find a way to block out the haters, or at least balance their negativity. Instead of questioning herself on the rest of the trip home, Kate thought about her motivation for doing what she was doing. She reminded herself that she loved it! She loved being part of her clients' growing businesses. She loved breeding cows. Trying to find a perfect genetic match in the hope of breeding increased production and anatomical perfection was exciting—it was her favourite challenge. Kate decided that, 'the only gauge she would use to determine success would be happy customers and a growing, profitable business. These were the things that were important. Really, the rest was a distraction and a waste of time and energy.'

From that point, Kate started implementing new strategies for maintaining her positivity and self-belief.

I started making follow-up calls to new customers for at least half of the time I was driving. This was great for two reasons. First, my new customers were generally excited and positive about the change they had made, and they believed in me and my business enough to make a change to Nexus. They were the positive voices I needed to hear to balance the negativity. Second, I had flagged that driving time was the time that I was most likely to let self-doubt rule my mind, so decreasing this time was very helpful. These simple changes quickly built new, positive habits that soon became automatic.

Kate says the important thing she learned during this time was to check-in with herself. 'Making changes to the way you approach situations, how you feel, or they direction you want to steer your mind, can only happen when you can identify what you want to change.'

THE MANICURED
LAWN FROM ABOVE

This is the story of a young girl growing up in small-town regional Victoria—how she came to be a role model for other young women, and to have a career and a small business in regional Australia. Her story is that you don't have to be in the big smoke to have an influence, or to have a satisfying work life.

This story is about me.

Truth be told, I reckon I started writing this book in my head when I was still a little girl. I'm not sure how old I was the first time I heard my mother telling me about her regret at not taking her education further. Mum grew up in rural Gippsland, on a dairy farm that was remote from town by the standards of the day. That same location is now a rural idyll on the edge of the suburban Latrobe Valley, but it was not viewed that way at the time.

Mum was educated at a tiny school until the equivalent of Year 8, common for the time. She then went on to do Year 9 by correspondence, as she wasn't able to access the high school in a larger town for various reasons. She wanted to train to work in mothercraft nursing with infants and small children. She didn't finish her correspondence year, and went on to be a shop assistant and then bookkeeper in town when she was old enough to board away from home. I heard that story many times in my childhood, usually in response to me complaining about school, or homework, or being unsure about my career path. I'm not sure if Mum even realises the impact that story had on me – or, indeed, if I realised it until I started writing the book.

I also clearly recall, on many occasions, as a small girl asking my parents why my brothers could be Cub scouts, but I had to join Brownies. I'm sure many girls asked this question. Mine was genuine. The boys seemed to be doing activities that I was more interested in. Despite its certain value to others, I didn't want to do a tea-making badge. I wanted to build billy-carts.

In a favourite story shared by my father and I, I finally got part of my way when, in the late 1970s, as a Girl Guide, my patrol leader and I convinced the authorities, including the Scouting District Commissioner (my Dad) that the Guide patrol I was part of should be able to enter the Scouts annual Billy Cart Derby. This event attracted Scouts from all over Gippsland and South-Eastern Melbourne, and had hundreds of participants. There were mixed views about adding 5 girls to this all-male tribe. We had to build a cart. We had to run through waterholes and carry the cart through creeks. We would get messy. We had to stop at check-points and answer general knowledge questions about Scouting, and undertake tasks like tying knots. The boys were quite okay with it, by the way. We were met with a mix of stares, shy laughter, wolf whistles and outright stunned silence at the starting line. I still have the photo my Mum took that day of our team lined up ready to race as 12- and 13-year-olds. Our grins could not be wiped away. Later that night when we walked on stage to collect our trophy for 1st prize in the Scouting Knowledge section, we were cheered. I'm still proud of that achievement. (Ironically, my husband was a Scout in the event. We didn't meet for many years after that. He clearly remembers that event though, and the award. He remembers that as a time when boys were simply considered as 'better', and how he and his mates vowed to do better next year so they could beat us if we came back. I'm glad I helped inspire them to aspire further! We laugh together now about how he never imagined marrying one of those Guides.)

Later, in 1983, I was completing my HSC. One night, at home with my parents, I was watching *Four Corners,* which featured a documentary. It was a piece of investigative journalism about the review of the Henderson Report, which had been undertaken in the mid-1970s, with regard to Australians living in poverty, and which had led to some very specific social reforms that still underpin some of our community welfare structures today—although it appears they are being dismantled.

The program was about a family, living in suburban Melbourne, who did not have enough money to live from week to week, and they spent the last few days of each week (pre pay-day), living on brown rice cooked with vegemite, and often with the mother not eating a main meal.

I was spellbound by this program; completely shocked out of my 17-year old's socks. I had never considered poverty or its implications, but that night, I couldn't get the family out of my head, because they were an average, everyday household, with Dad working, and kids aspiring to go to university etc.—just like all the people in my street and in my classroom.

In my very working-class family—1 parent a migrant and the other 3rd generation Gippslander, with a dual income household, 3 older siblings all in good jobs—it just seemed there was never a reason for me to question our social fabric.

That single program, as it turns out, also changed my life. I had been going to train as a secondary teacher majoring in history and geography – but that night, I made a decision to train in social welfare and community development, (not that I knew what to call my choice at the time) and essentially, I built my career in those sectors.

I went on to finish HSC, graduated with an Associate Diploma in Welfare Studies in 1986, and went on to complete a Graduate Diploma in Business, majoring in Labour Management Relations in 1992. Among other things, these qualifications enhanced my ability to carry out the tasks handed to me in my various jobs, and have given me a theoretical base from which to understand some aspects of the world around me.

My earlier work centered on the public sector; children's welfare, rehabilitation of injured workers, intellectual disability services, and managing regional agencies. It just so happens that I was able to do all these things while still being based in a regional city, which was very rewarding for me, personally.

In 2009, I left the region to take up a Chief Executive role in a state-wide peak body for local government in Victoria. I remained in that role for just over 4 years, living in inner Melbourne during the week, and returning home to Gippsland on weekends.

I'm proud that in that time I was an example of a woman in local government leadership, and that I was instrumental in seeking and winning State Government funding to embark on an ambitious project to increase women's representation at the local elected level.

As a result of the hard work we undertook in this project, in the October 2012 council elections, around 660 candidates were women, which is about a third of the 2004 people who put their hand up for one of the 631 vacancies—a first.

Around 80% of wards had at least one woman in the running, and the result was 213 women leaning into the decision-making table in all councils across the State. Every council in Victoria, for the first time, had at least one woman councillor. Of these 213 councillors, 29 were mayors—the highest percentage in Victoria's history, and a national record.

By no means does this exclusively mean they were better councillors or contributed to better decisions. The point is, they were there. They better represented the 51% of our population that is female. They used many of the services they were making decisions about, in ways which men never had, nor would. It was the first time in our nation that local governance had been so representative.

In concluding that time, I went back to university for a third time, and undertook post-graduate studies in workplace and organisational coaching, and executive coaching. While doing so, I worked back in the public service and in an agricultural research agency in a leadership role in Gippsland.

It was at that time that I reassessed my deepest personal values. I discovered the incongruence I felt between who I was, and the work I was doing. While studying and working in the public sector, I made my decision to start my own consulting practice, and to write this book. In November 2015, I got started on the newest chapter of my life, just prior to turning 50.

For me, work has often been a 'vocation', not a job. I have mostly chosen jobs that I know I will enjoy and give me satisfaction; therefore, work is not a chore, and working long hours has been quite comfortable. I accept that it has been, at times, par for the course in the senior roles I have occupied.

While never having needed them myself, I fully support and endorse paid parental leave schemes, and I rejoice the many companies who offer work-based childcare for the women who want to use it. On their own, these schemes are not enough to make the economy truly effective. Our social structures and views of the multiple roles of women in society must also change, before those workplace initiatives can truly make a difference. I believe that's what my elder sisters were on about when they first challenged the world to think differently about women.

My most important influences have come from other women – teaching me what it means to be a woman in the broadest sense, including women like my mother, and others, such as particular teachers, colleagues, and women I chose to 'mirror' and learn from. There are several mentors I still regularly have contact with, and who have become good friends.

My choices about life and career have meant I feel like I'm parasailing. While I'm safely tethered to my work and my regional life, I have a big view of the wider landscape and all my horizons from a great height. Hovering above, with all my experiences, means I'm not restricting myself or my opportunities any more.

In turn, it's now my time to mentor other women. I provide formal mentoring programs on a paid basis as part of my practice, after many years of mentoring people in my paid and voluntary jobs. This book is my effort to mentor more broadly, and to keep the conversation going.

I do hope your spade is now sharpened as a result of reading the book.

Now, go and start cutting through.

WORKS CITED

Introudction

1   Hutchinson, B. in Sandberg, S. & Scovell, N. (2015). *Lean In: Women, Work and the Will to Lead.* Ebury.

2   Regional Policy Advisory Committee. (2013). *Research into Education Aspiration for Regional Victoria – Full Report.* State of Victoria.

3   Porter Dawn (2015). *Lean Out.* Repeater Books. London UK.

Chapter 1

1   http://www.lgfocus.com.au/editions/2015-09/breaking-the-grass-ceiling.php

2   Pippos, Angela (2017). *Breaking the Mould: Taking a Hammer to Sexism in Sport.* Affirm Press. Melbourne

3   https://www.vwt.org.au/breakthrough-2016/breaking-grass-ceiling/

4   Alston, M. (2000). *Breaking through the grass ceiling: Women, power and leadership in agricultural organisations.* Routledge.

Chapter 2

1   Gurría, A. (2014). Session 1 – *The global economy: strengthening growth and job creation.* Remarks made at the G20 Leaders Summit, Brisbane, 15-16 November 2014. Online: https://www.oecd.org/g20/summits/brisbane/the-global-economy-strengthening-growth-and-job-creation.htm

2   Ledbetter, B. (2014). *A Values Approach to Advancing Women in Leadership: Using Talent Management to Change the Equation.* Graziadio Business Review, Vol 17 Issue 3. Graziadio School of Business and Management. Pepperdine University

3   Lees, K. (17 November 2015). *Closing the gender pay gap: only 80 years to go*. Australian Institute of Management blog. Online: http://www.aim.com.au/blog/closing-gender-pay-gap-only-80-years-go?utm_source=marketo&utm_medium=email&utm_campaign=nov-enews-memb&mkt_tok=3RkMMJWWfF9wsRouv6%2FPZKXonjHpfsX56ekoWae2lMI%2F0ER3fOvrPUfGjI4JScdmI%2BSLDwEYGJlv6SgFTbTHMbF10LgEWXc%3D

4   Silverstein, M. & Sayre, K. (2009). The Female Economy. *Harvard Business Review*. September issue. Online: https://hbr.org/2009/09/the-female-economy

5   Noland, M. & Moran, T. (2016). Study: Firms With More Women in the C-suite Are More Profitable. *Harvard Business Review*. Online: https://hbr.org/2016/02/study-firms-with-more-women-in-the-c-suite-are-more-profitable

6   McGaughy, M. (2016). *Women In Leadership Dominate Emerging Markets....And It Pays Off*. Forbes May 12, 2016. Online: http://www.forbes.com/sites/michaelmcgaughy/2016/05/12/women-leaders-another-reason-to-invest-in-emerging-markets/#43a78a7b2420

7   Krawcheck, S. (14 December 2015). *We're Entering the Golden Age of Female Entrepreneurship – and It'll Be Amazing*. LinkedIn blog. Online: https://www.linkedin.com/pulse/big-idea-2016-were-entering-golden-age-female-itll-sallie-krawcheck?trk=hp-feed-article-title-channel-add

8   Bender-Phelps, S. *Boomer Brain Drain = Historic Opportunities for Women*. Online http://bizcatalyst360.com/boomer-brain-drain-historic-opportunities-for-women/?__scoop_post=cfa96c40-43fe-11e6-b9fe-90b11c40440d&__scoop_topic=5064893#__scoop_post=cfa96c40-43fe-11e6-b9fe-90b11c40440d&__scoop_topic=5064893 Accessed 13 August 2016.

Chapter 3

1   Assistant Governor (Economic) Reserve Bank of Australia in her speech to the ACT Launch of the Women in Economics Network Canberra – 20 March 2017.

2   National Seniors Australia. http://www.nationalseniors.com.au/
     be-informed/research/publications/my-generation Accessed 13
     August 2016.

3   Wittenberg-Cox, A. (2016). *What Work Looks Like for Women
     in Their 50s. Harvard Business Review*. online https://hbr.
     org/2016/04/what-work-looks-like-for-women-in-their-50s?

4   Accenture. (2016). *Getting to Equal – How Digital is Helping Close
     the Gender Gap at Work*, P 3.

5   Perera, G. *China On Our Doorstep* http://gihanperera.com/blog.
     html/page/7/ accessed 13 August 2016.

Chapter 5

1   Bridge, R. Author of *Ambition: Why It's Good to Want More and
     How to Get It.*

Chapter 6

1   Banaji, M. & Greenwald, A. (2013). *Blindspot*. Delacorte Press,
     New York.

2   Jenkins, L (2015). *Unconscious Gender Bias: Everyone's Issue*.
     Huffington Post. 27 May 2015. http://www.huffingtonpost.com/
     lisa-marie-jenkins/unconscious-gender-bias-e_b_7447524.html

3   Salles, N. (2016) *How Female Leaders Accidentally Hold Themselves
     Back*. LinkedIn blog. Online: https://www.linkedin.com/pulse/
     how-female-leaders-accidentally-hold-themselves-back-nathalie-
     salles?trk=hp-feed-article-title-like

4   Sankar, C ,(2015) *The Confidence Factor for Women in Leadership:
     Conversations with Women CEOs & Leaders*. I.L Press.

5   Gevinti, N. (2015). *How Much Are You Contributing to Your Own
     Glass Ceiling?* LinkedIn blog. Online: https://www.linkedin.com/
     pulse/how-much-you-contributing-your-own-glass-ceiling-natha-
     lie-gevinti

Chapter 7

1   http://www2.psych.ubc.ca/~schaller/528Readings/Festinger1954.
     pdf

Chapter 8

1   http://www.inc.com/issie-lapowsky/malcolm-gladwell-start-as-a-big-fish.html

2   Dweck, C. (2006). *Mindset: How You Can Fulfil Your Potentia*l. Constable & Robinson, London.

3   http://psych.fullerton.edu/jmearns/rotter.htm

4   Brands, R. & Fernandez-Matteo, I. (2017). Women Are Less Likely to Apply for Executive Roles if They've Been Rejected Before. *Harvard Business Review*. Accessed online: https://hbr.org/2017/02/women-are-less-likely-to-apply-for-executive-roles-if-theyve-been-rejected-before

Chapter 9

1   Kahneman, D. & Tversky, A. (1979). "Prospect Theory: An Analysis of Decision under Risk". *Econometrica*. 47 (2): 263. doi:10.2307/1914185. ISSN 0012-9682.

2   http://brenebrown.com/?s=fear&submit=

3   http://www.therichest.com/business/how-fear-of-success-might-be-holding-you-back/

4   Anderson, Je. 2015. *Impact: How to Build Your Personal Brand for the Connection Economy*. Amazon.

5   https://margiewarrell.com/risk-more-rejection/

6   https://www.ted.com/talks/ruth_chang_how_to_make_hard_choices

7   Loomes, G. & Sugden, R. (1982), "Regret theory: An alternative theory of rational choice under uncertainty", Economic Journal, 92(4), 805–824.

8   https://www.forbes.com/sites/jeffboss/2016/05/22/embrace-curiosity-4-ways-questioning-makes-you-a-better-leader/#32d-f6a37b640

9   http://www.gordontraining.com/free-workplace-articles/learning-a-new-skill-is-easier-said-than-done/#

10 https://www.internationalwomensday.com/Theme

11 http://www.huffingtonpost.com/evie-hantzopoulos/help-all-youth-be-bold_b_5627909.html

12 https://www.forbes.com/sites/dailymuse/2011/12/21/get-visible-the-secrets-of-self-promotion/#41dfe59a1e6c

13 http://www.latrobewomeninbusiness.com.au/

Chapter 10

1 nderson, J. & Chown, K. (2015). *Connect*. Full Stop Design, Editing, Publishing.

Chapter 11

1 Coutu, D. (2008). Obama's Cautionary Tale: Pick Your Mentors With Care. *Harvard Business Review*. May 23, 2008 https://hbr.org/2008/05/obamas-cautionary-tale-pick-yo

2 Aarons-Mele, M. (2015) For Women, Aspiration and Confidence Erode in Mid-Career (graphic) in *Harvard Business Review* May 18 2015. Accessed online https://hbr.org/visual-library/2015/05/for-women-aspiration-and-confidence-erode-in-mid-career

3 Murphy W. (2016). How Women (and Men) Can Find Role Models When None Are Obvious. in *Harvard Business Review* June 1 2016. Accessed online https://hbr.org/2016/06/how-women-and-men-can-find-role-models-when-none-are-obvious

4 Management Mentors (2015). "9 Benefits of Mentoring That Go Beyond Traditional ROI". www.management-mentors.com

5 Staszkow, B. "4 Ways Executive Leadership Development Coaching Improves Your Performance", sourced online http://bit.ly/1X-pZAmm

Chapter 12

1 http://www.latrobevalleyexpress.com.au/story/3908650/willow-grove-mums-help-secure-state-wide-funding-for-kindergartens/

2 http://www.farmonline.com.au/story/4428516/unsung-bush-heroes-in-spotlight-for-australian-of-the-year-awards/

ABOUT THE AUTHOR

Maree is a coach, mentor, facilitator, and writer. Maree's passion is to help people aspire beyond that of which they think they are capable. Curiosity is her mantra, and she encourages her clients to test ideas, explore new concepts, and ask questions they've always been hesitant to ask.

Maree is an Associate Certified Coach, with tertiary qualifications in executive and organisational coaching, business and social welfare. She works with corporate organisations, not-for-profits, board members, organisational teams and individuals. She is a Fellow of the Australian Institute of Management, and a Graduate member of the Australian Institute of Company Directors.

Maree is an experienced not for profit, government and community leader, board member, and small business owner. She is a creator of strong relationships across multiple stakeholder groups, and a proven effective broker of partnerships with more than 30 years' experience, including as a CEO and Chair in the public and for-purpose (not-for-profit) domains.

Because she is passionate about community leadership, Maree is an active Rotarian and enjoys supporting international and local projects—especially projects aimed at advancing and improving the lives of girls and women.

Maree's fundamental belief in the power of education to change lives led her to become a member of the Victorian Adult, Community and Further Education Board for over five years. Her commitment to developing regional Victoria resulted in Maree being appointed by the Victorian Government to the Regional Development Advisory Committee.

To find out more about how Maree can help you, go to www.mareemcpherson.com and sign up to her network. You can also e-mail her via hello@mareemcpherson.com.au

www.ingramcontent.com/pod-product-compliance
Lightning Source LLC
Chambersburg PA
CBHW062005200326
41519CB00017B/4682